Feel Good

Easy Steps to Health and Happiness

Dr. Ameet Aggarwal ND

ISBN: 1490310126
ISBN-13: 9781490310121
Library of Congress Control Number: 2013910229
CreateSpace Independent Publishing Platform
North Charleston, South Carolina

I dedicate this book to my family and to the amazing teachers, staff and everyone else at The Canadian College of Naturopathic Medicine (CCNM). Thank you for your contagious inspiration for life!

ACKNOWLEDGMENTS

Thank you Trixie, Giulia, Allison, Rubina, Steve, Paola, Marnee, Shelan, Anoma, Karen, Nita, Cheeko, Jess, Louisa and all my friends for making this book possible. Thank you Daniel of Dlightgraphics for the illustrations. Thank you to my family for always being there for me. Thank you to the entire team of FIMAFRICA and all volunteers for your support and inspiration - I hope we can continue this amazing work. Thank you to all my patients for being with me on this journey and helping me learn so much from you. Thank you to all my teachers at the Canadian College of Naturopathic Medicine for inspiring me so much on this path of healing, and to my gestalt teachers for awakening my understanding of transforming consciousness. Transforming consciousness is a new path that we all must take, I believe, in order to uncover our strengths as well as our vulnerabilities, which is where our true power begins.

CONTENTS

Online consultations, training, group healing seminars and healing journey safaris available from www.drameet.com

PART 2

Online consultations, training, group healing seminars and healing journey safaris available
from www.drameet.com

PREFACE

Who am I, and why did I write this book?

I am a naturopathic doctor and practice a form of psychotherapy known as gestalt therapy. I help a lot of people with emotional problems through counseling and also by improving the health of their bodies. My job is both satisfying and frustrating because, as you've probably noticed, people with physical and emotional problems have a very tough time getting better.

Some take a lot of medicines or nutritional and herbal supplements and yet never resolve their emotional issues. Others go for counseling or read positive mindset books but never heal their bodies. This book shows you how to combine holistic medicine with positive thinking, since it is necessary to heal both your mind and body together in order to recover completely.

This book combines my personal experience and proven therapies I use with my patients to bring long-term relief from sadness, emotional pain, depression, anxiety, fear, irritability, stress, dissatisfaction, fatigue, and many other emotional issues. I have personally benefitted from these techniques and so have many of my patients who are now happier and emotionally stronger.

Even though the focus of this book is your emotional well-being, by following my advice you can resolve numerous other ailments, including digestive issues, hormonal problems, skin issues, obesity, asthma, joint problems, and other chronic diseases, since a large focus of this book is about reducing inflammation, stress and imbalance in your body – the major causes of most chronic diseases.

Here is what you will learn in this book.

Part 1 introduces different factors which affect your emotions. You'll learn how physical factors affect your emotional experiences. I'll show you how stressful experiences have a long term impact on emotional wellbeing and I give you powerful mental techniques to heal from stress and painful emotional experiences. You'll find out how to resolve turbulent emotions, change negative thoughts and beliefs, rewire your brain and develop more positive thoughts and habits to become more emotionally resilient and remain well for longer.

Part 2 teaches you how your body affects your mind. I go into detail about your brain chemicals and how organs other than your brain play a key role in emotional well-being. This is something which doctors usually don't discuss or treat. You learn how diet, lifestyle and environmental toxins affect your body and mind, rendering you prone to recurrent bouts of emotional instability. You will learn to create balance throughout your body and heal the root cause of your emotional ill health using herbs, diet, lifestyle changes, yoga, breathing techniques and other powerful therapies. These therapies reduce the likelihood of you relapsing into emotional un-wellness. They reinforce your mental strength, build emotional resilience and help you remain healthy. You can read Part 2 before Part 1 or interchange between the two parts because it is vital to heal your mind and your body concurrently.

Part 3 discusses how energy affects your mind and your body and why energetic healing, counseling and psychotherapy can be so important to your long term wellbeing. You will also understand how to use different homeopathic remedies, Bach flower remedies, nutritional supplements, acupuncture points and herbal remedies so that you can treat the root cause of your issues and remain healthy.

Even though I use the terms anxiety and depression liberally throughout this book, I have written it for anyone who wants to feel better. The advice in this book is useful for anyone who wants to be less stressed, heal from past stressful experiences, or just wants to feel more energized, healthy and positive. We all experience difficult situations in our lives that we need to heal from.

Unfortunately, surveys indicate that many people avoid seeking treatment or even refuse to admit that they have a problem because of the negative stigma associated with emotional problems. Some people think they will be judged as being weak or incapable of coping with life, not realizing that they have a very treatable condition that stems from very reasonable and non-shameful causes. Some people think their depressed emotions are part of their core personality and that they do not have emotional issues, so they do not seek help. Sadly, many of these people do not get help in time and let their life deteriorate further, sometimes even to the point of suicide.

It is not the goal of this book to replace medical advice. My goal is to help you treat the root cause of your emotional issues and resolve unfinished emotional experiences that contribute to your current emotional state, and to enable you to make healthier decisions for your road to wellbeing. I also hope that psychiatrists will read this book and look beyond mere medications to help people feel better. You might find that by using the techniques in this book you will require less medication. Please be responsible with your health and consult with a qualified professional before changing any of your medications or using some of the therapies described here.

If you like what you read in this book and would like to train with me, have a consultation, go on a healing journey safari, or have me work with your organization, please contact me. If you are a health care practitioner and would like continuing education credits, feel welcome to listen to my webinars. I'll also be posting some inspirational quotes and health tips online. You can find all this information on **www.facebook.com/DrameetND** and **www. drameet.com**.

Welcome to a happier life!

ABOUT THE AUTHOR

Dr. Ameet Aggarwal ND was born in Nanyuki, a little town on the foothills of Mount Kenya, right on the equator. He moved to Canada to pursue university, and has travelled through various countries, touching the lives of many people through his intuitive understanding of people's deeper emotions. He graduated from The Canadian College of Naturopathic Medicine (CCNM) in 2006 and also trained with The Gestalt Institute of Toronto for 4 years. In addition to naturopathic medicine and gestalt therapy, he practices Bowen therapy and family constellations systemic theory. He has combined these specialties to provide the most comprehensive care to his patients. Always aiming to treat the root cause, resolve emotional causes of disease and promote long term health, Ameet honours the principles of holistic and integrated medicine.

After graduating from CCNM, Ameet practiced in Vancouver and White Rock Canada for a year. His passion for naturopathic medicine and homeopathy led him to start the charity The Foundation for Integrated Medicine in Africa (FIMAFRICA), and head to Kenya to provide naturopathic medicine to remote villages living without health care. He supervises students and doctors from around the world who volunteer with FIMAFRICA, teaching them clinical skills, homeopathy and integrated medicine. He also provides volunteers with personal growth sessions using gestalt therapy, so that they become more self aware, empowered and better practitioners for their patients.

Ameet runs team building and stress reduction workshops for corporations and NGOs using gestalt therapy, and did a workshop for UNICEF with participants from around the globe. These workshops provide a completely new approach to team building and stress reduction. Participants go through exercises which enhance self awareness, heal belief systems and encourage them to take risks in new ways of communication and relating to other people. After the workshops, people feel they have more confidence and can resolve conflicts better. Organizations notice improved trust, communication and respect within their teams.

Ameet also runs health and emotional wellbeing retreats in exotic locations in Africa. They combine safaris, beach and healing so that you can have deeply transforming experiences while on holiday. He currently practices in Kenya and avails himself to people around the world through online consults and seminars.

PART 1

INTRODUCTION

It is more important to know what sort of person has a disease than to know what sort of disease a person has.
~ Hippocrates (460– 377 B C)

"**M**Y HEALTH WAS not the same as it was before, I could feel it. Even worse, my emotions were hitting rock bottom. I would lie in bed or on the floor, sometimes crying needlessly and feeling pity for myself. Crying would somehow bring me relief, but the gloominess never shifted. I didn't feel enthusiastic anymore. I had no motivation or confidence to do new things. My energy was not like it used to be. What I used to enjoy in the past didn't feel like so much fun anymore. Was there something wrong with me? What was wrong with me? What had changed me? I felt awkward talking to certain people because I thought they would not like me. I also felt guilty very easily. Why did I feel so guilty? I had to hide my tears sometimes when walking in the streets...tears of emotional pain for sometimes unknown reasons. Had someone told me I was depressed, I would have resisted, since I knew I was a stronger person, and in my opinion, depressed people needed medications and I doubted I needed medication. I just had to figure out how to get out of this state…"

Do any of these feelings sound familiar to you? They might not. Even though I don't like to admit it, this was me, struggling with declining health and feelings of sadness, anxiety, and possible depression after a long stressful period in my life. Luckily, because of my training and tremendous help from my colleagues, I found my way out of this dark cloud. Using the techniques I have described in this book, I can truly say that I am much healthier and happier now; I feel more motivated, lighter, sure of myself; and I have much healthier personal relationships. I now even run training seminars, emotional healing and team building workshops and health retreats in exotic locations in Africa.

FACTORS THAT AFFECT EMOTIONAL HEALTH

E VEN THOUGH I was struggling emotionally with a difficult situation in my life, I quickly realized it was not only *external experiences* that were affecting my wellbeing. The things I ate and my activity levels were strongly influencing my mental and physical health. I was very vulnerable to health issues, fatigue, anxiety and depressive thoughts. It was only after I started changing my diet and lifestyle, exercising and taking herbs and supplements that I began to realize the strong physiological connection with my emotions. My lifestyle habits were having a major impact on my body's chemistry and my body's chemistry was directly affecting my brain chemistry. I also worked with various therapists to release emotional experiences from my past, which were affecting the way I looked at the world and hindering me from enjoying my present life.

Because of my personal experience, my training, and experience with numerous patients, I really want you to look at the following areas of your life if you are struggling with health problems or your emotions and are trying to gain emotional peace and strength:

1. *Has there been any physically or emotionally traumatic event in your life?*

If there has been emotional trauma or stressful events in your life, the limbic part of your brain remains stressed even years after the trauma, and an unconscious part of you never fully recovers. You end up going through life permanently affected by the event. It becomes a part of your story. Therapies such as counseling, psychotherapy, homeopathic medicines, or Bach flower remedies, all of which I discuss in later chapters, help release emotional trauma from your conscious and unconscious mind and from your limbic brain. By releasing emotional trauma, you begin to experience life from a place of strength, liveliness, and authenticity.

2. *Is a biological or chemical imbalance affecting your emotions?*

Your mind is affected by neurotransmitters, hormones, and other chemical messengers floating around your body. Neurotransmitters and hormones are directly influenced by nutrients in the foods you eat, environmental toxins, and also by the health of your different organs. In the next chapters, you will learn how your liver, adrenal glands, thyroid gland, and digestive system affect your mood. You will also learn how to heal these organs and use the right foods, nutrients, and herbs to correct the balance of your body. Doing this will enhance your wellbeing with long-lasting results, and reduce the ups and downs many people go through when they rely only on temporary fixes.

3. *Is there a stressful situation in your life or a lifestyle choice that is interfering with your ability to heal?*

Chronic stress is the fastest way to break a person. Being around critical, aggressive, or emotionally abusive people keeps you in a perpetual state of stress. If you are in a stressful situation, whether socially or at work, you need to take immediate steps to move out of it or seek help to cope with it in a healthier and more empowered way. Equally, you need to exercise regularly to help your body recover from stress and learn to avoid certain unhealthy activities. Everyday activities that you may think are helping you relax can actually exacerbate your stress levels. Things like drinking too much alcohol or watching too much TV interfere with your chances of recovering fully. Abusing narcotic drugs, gossiping about others, talking negatively about life, hanging out with people who do not promote your well-being, spending too much time at work without caring for yourself, and doing things that do not help you feel good are also ways you stress your mind and your body without knowing it.

Unnecessary and unhealthy habits interfere with emotional healing and take up valuable time that could be spent improving your health. Try and fill every spare moment or idle time you have in the day with healthier activities, such as exercise, positive conversations, reading inspirational books, yoga, meditation, breathing exercises, and social activities that enhance your sense of wellbeing rather than make you sick and disappointed later on. In later chapters, I show you some easy *feel-good* exercises you can do to fill up your day and heal your emotions.

"Jane" was a thirty-four-year-old patient of mine suffering from chronic depression. She had been a volunteer in Somalia and had suffered stressful conflicts with her colleagues. She suffered from insomnia and binge eating as part of her depression. She had also suffered from chronic headaches since she was a child and had experienced her father being abusive toward her mother when she was growing up. The emotional trauma of her childhood had left her feeling vulnerable during conflicts, which led her to back away from standing up for herself as an adult and increased her stress at work.

In Jane's case, her emotional family history played a huge role in her susceptibility to fear and depression. At the same time, her chronic stress had depleted her adrenal glands (adrenal gland health is covered extensively in upcoming chapters), leaving her exhausted and unable to overcome emotional issues. In addition, her binge eating of a lot of starchy foods, combined with her stress, caused her blood-sugar, cortisol, and insulin levels to become unstable, leaving her exasperated and prone to chemical imbalances that affected her mood and her health. As part of Jane's healing journey, we encouraged her to eat healthy foods, which improved the level of brain chemicals in her blood. We resolved many of her previous emotional traumas using psychotherapy and energy based medicines (homeopathic and Bach flower remedies, discussed in later chapters), helping her to release the traumatic experiences that were still influencing her unconscious mind and affecting her behavior. We also built up her adrenal gland health using herbs and nutritional supplements so that her chemical imbalances were further corrected and stabilized for longer periods of time.

Jane's case was a typical case of depression that was resolved using a multi-angle, comprehensive holistic approach. She had to address her emotional history, her diet, as well as her physical health in order to feel emotionally well for longer periods of time.

The approach of resolving emotional experiences, restoring your body's optimal physical state and engaging in healthy daily activities is the cornerstone of building a foundation for emotional strength. By healing the root cause, you do not suppress symptoms, are less dependent on medication, and you will likely feel deeply better for much longer periods of time.

THE EFFECTS OF EMOTIONAL EXPERIENCES

All emotional experiences begin a physiological process in your body. For every act, emotion, and expression of love, self-love, self-forgiveness, and forgiveness toward another, your body reengages toward another physiological process, closer to its original process, its healthiest process...
~ Dr. Ameet Aggarwal ND

E MOTIONAL AND TRAUMATIC events have a long-term impact on our health, be it a relationship breakup, parents fighting, divorces, a significant loss, financial difficulties, death of a loved one, or some other factor. Biologically speaking, your brain has the ability to create new neural connections based on what you experience. This ability is what doctors call **neuroplasticity**. Significant events alter the neural pathways in our brain, causing new nerve connections to be formed in order to cope with the stress and to anticipate similar events that may occur in the future. These new neural connections alter your perception of

Online consultations, training, group healing seminars and healing journey safaris available from www.drameet.com

the world and of yourself so that things *do not appear the same as they used to be when you were vibrant and happy.* These new neural pathways also **alter the entire physiology of your body**, causing organs to function differently and causing chemicals, enzymes, and hormones to be made in different amounts, both of which directly affect your health and hinder your ability to recover emotionally.

Brain Connections Change Due to Neuroplasticity.

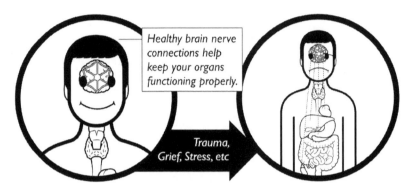

After stress and trauma, your brain develops unhealthy nerve connections to compensate for the stress. This has an unhealthy affect on your organs, causing emotional problems, certain diseases, changes in the way you see life and changes in behaviour.

Sometimes you might not even be aware that a particular emotional event has such a profound effect on you. If left unresolved or tucked away hidden under a stone in the back of your mind, the effects of these experiences continue to affect your mind and your body consciously, subconsciously, or unconsciously. This creates what I call **emotional holding patterns, or EHPs**, where your mind and body remain affected and continue to respond to emotional experiences as if they were still occurring, even though they might have finished. I believe that when the emotions surrounding your experience are too large for your mind to cope with, or if the EHPs go on for too long, a part of your mind shuts down by going into depression in order to conserve energy for expected experiences. Depression is also partly due to a lack of trust in your environment based on previous stressful experiences and is also a state of exhaustion your body reaches when it can no longer cope with stress.

The chronic stress from EHPs taxes your stress-adapting organs such as your adrenal glands and thyroid glands. **Overstressed and under-functioning adrenal glands are a leading cause** of chronic anxiety, depression, and other health problems. You need to resolve or discharge EHPs in order to correct the altered neural pathways created in your brain, stop their negative effect on your body, and to give your brain a rest, rather than let it remain stressed from past events. Resolving stress and EHPs is also important because physically stressed organs in your body use up many more nutrients and produce more toxins than in a calm and relaxed body. When nutrients begin to run out in your body, your brain and other organs no longer have enough neurotransmitters and hormones to keep you happy and healthy.

"John" was thirty years old and had bipolar disorder, where he fluctuated between depression and manic or hyperactive and anxious states. The root cause of his condition was a traumatic divorce between his parents when he was seven years old and an unstable home environment while he was growing up. Because he experienced continuous stress as a young child, his whole development from childhood to adulthood was that of a stressed person. The constant threat and instability left his mind no way to feel safe, and he began to develop coping mechanisms that were dysfunctional to his body's natural rhythm.

John's treatment involved resolving the emotional pain from his memories using psychotherapy and homeopathic medicines and also stabilizing his adrenal glands, which were out of balance due to the chronic anxiety he grew up with (we will cover homeopathic medicines and adrenal glands in later chapters). With counseling, he realized how much stress he still carried due to his strained childhood. With counseling, he also developed the awareness and the power to deal with his anxiety and reconsider his adult surroundings with less stress and more peace. He felt safer trusting his external environment. After a few sessions of counseling and naturopathic medicine, John's condition completely resolved, and he had no more manic episodes. This was because he not only healed his body, but managed to resolve his emotional holding patterns.

Negative events from your past hinder your authentic expression and alter the way you interact with others. As you continue to live your life in a compensated way, you perpetuate the negative feelings you carry with you. Emotional healing is an opportunity to awaken the healthier and happier self within you and interact with others and with the world in a more positive way that inevitably gives you more positive experiences. As you recover emotionally from past events, you will begin to feel more confident and open in your life. With better health, you can gift yourself a more empowered and positive life.

Discharging and resolving stress and EHPs is possible through counseling, psychotherapy, talking to a friend, resolving the conflict and forgiving. Some of the best therapies I've experienced which release EHPs include gestalt therapy, neuro-linguistic programming (NLP), emotional freedom technique (EFT), eye movement desensitization and reprocessing (EMDR, a type of psychotherapy), meditation and other mind-body techniques, which I cover in later chapters. Homeopathic medicines and Bach flower remedies, covered in their own separate chapters, are energetic medicines that are also very effective in resolving EHPs.

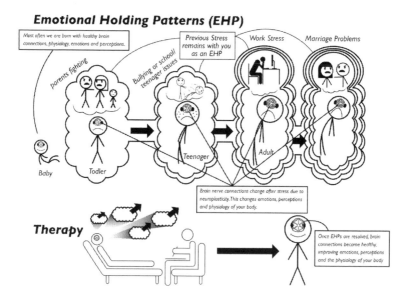

Emotional Holding Patterns (EHP)

HOW YOUR PHYSICAL BODY AFFECTS EMOTIONAL HEALTH

"To keep the body in good health is a duty...otherwise we shall not be able to keep our mind strong and clear."
~ Buddha

I SPENT A LOT of time going for psychotherapy and emotional healing with different therapists. It all worked reasonably well; however, there was always an underlying discomfort in my emotions. It was only when I started exercising regularly, treating myself with nutritional supplements and ate foods that were good for me that I began to see permanent results with my emotional strength.

Emotional *dis-ease* is often due to an imbalance of chemicals (neurotransmitters) in your body and in your brain. Most people assume that emotional problems are due solely to chemical imbalances in the brain. Neurotransmitters, however, are produced and balanced by many organs in your body, not only your brain, and mood fluctuations are often a signal of something wrong happening with one of your other organs.

"Helen" came to see me with insomnia, anxiety, and painful and irregular menstrual periods. She was having too much sugar and drank three cups of coffee a day. The coffee was interfering with her liver function, which was affecting her sleep and her hormones (I explain more on this in the chapter "*Your Liver and Emotional Wellbeing*"). The sugar and coffee were also reducing her *feel-good neurotransmitters* by ruining her adrenal glands and digestive system, which I explain in later chapters. Her lack of sleep was leaving her exhausted and making her anxiety worse. She ate very few vegetables, which starved her body of good nutrients and damaged her digestive system further, making her health even worse.

We changed her diet by removing coffee and sugar, and increasing vegetables and protein-rich foods such as fish and chicken. We cleansed her liver using herbs and other methods described later in this book. The results were astounding. Her menstrual periods became regular, her menstrual pains disappeared completely, her anxiety vanished, and healthy sleep patterns returned within three weeks. Not only that, her energy levels and concentration improved tremendously, and she was given a promotion at work. Her headaches, which she hadn't brought to my attention, had also vanished. This is achieving optimal health. Improving your diet and restoring your organ health can have amazing benefits in your life.

"We must turn to nature itself, to the observations of the body in health and in disease to learn the truth."
~ Hippocrates

The organs apart from your brain that play an essential role in emotional stability are your *adrenal glands, thyroid gland, digestive system,* and *liver.* These organ systems are also crucial to the foundation of your overall health. Keeping them healthy prevents and treats many other diseases, including arthritis, hormonal imbalances, ovarian cysts, fibroids, asthma, eczema, digestive issues, and several other chronic health problems.

There are many factors that directly affect the health of all your organs and the levels of neurotransmitters in your body and therefore influence your emotions. Here are a few:

- Nutrient and vitamin deficiencies, such as vitamin B3, vitamin B6, vitamin B12, vitamin C, folic acid, zinc, essential fatty acids (EFAs), and other nutrients that affect mental health.

- Poor diets, such as too many simple carbohydrates and sugars or too little protein and vegetables.

- Insufficient nutrient absorption because of a malfunctioning digestive system.

- Food intolerances and allergies.

- The amount of exercise you do. Regular exercise reduces depression and anxiety by increasing neurotransmitters in your body and increasing oxygenation of your brain and your organs.

- Blood-sugar balance. Unstable blood sugar often causes feelings of anxiety or depression, especially when not enough sugar feeds your brain.

- Hormonal imbalances caused by external estrogens, birth control pills, and water toxicity.

- Environmental and heavy metal toxicity such as lead, copper, mercury, aluminum, pesticides, and chemical toxicity.

In the upcoming chapters, you will learn how to remedy these factors and regain control of your physical and emotional wellbeing.

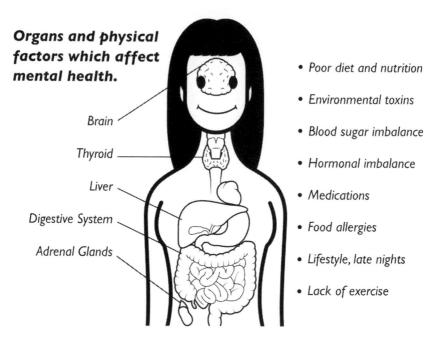

Organs and physical factors which affect mental health.

Brain

Thyroid

Liver

Digestive System

Adrenal Glands

- *Poor diet and nutrition*

- *Environmental toxins*

- *Blood sugar imbalance*

- *Hormonal imbalance*

- *Medications*

- *Food allergies*

- *Lifestyle, late nights*

- *Lack of exercise*

WHAT IS ANXIETY AND DEPRESSION?

*"Just like the unseen currents create winds, which you can feel,
which move a leaf, which you can see, so do unseen thoughts create emotions, which you can feel, which create disease or healing,
which you can see. We are all nature..."*
~ Dr. Ameet Aggarwal ND

I DISLIKE USING THE word *depression* because it has such a heavy and permanent feel to it, and it comes with its own stigma. The word depression doesn't seem to help anyone get over their emotional state and sometimes makes people feel worse when they are labeled with it. I like to say it is not a *solution-oriented* label. Emotional *difficulty* is a better word because it feels more like a temporary situation, so I use it interchangeably with the words anxiety and depression.

Depression, anxiety, and other mental illnesses are diagnosed by doctors according to the *Diagnostic and Statistical Manual of Mental Disorders* (DSM-V). In this manual, different labels are given to different mental conditions, depending on the symptoms a person has and on the intensity and frequency of these symptoms. Labels given to people include *depression, anxiety, obsessive-compulsive disorder, major depression, seasonal affective disorder, generalized anxiety disorder, paranoia, bipolar, schizophrenia, post-traumatic stress disorder,* and others.

Similar symptoms do, of course, exist across different labels. For example, people with generalized anxiety disorder and major depression both experience symptoms of anxiety, although the frequency and intensity of symptoms in each label differ. Similarly, people with obsessive-compulsive disorder and generalized anxiety disorder both experience varying degrees of paranoia and anxiety, just in different amounts and with different resulting behaviors.

Even though different mental conditions are given different names, many of them share similar chemical imbalances. This similarity means that different mood disorders are actually similar processes occurring in the body with different triggers and different levels of intensity. This being said, try not to get emotionally attached to a diagnosis that a doctor might give you. The root cause, the affected organ system and your individuality are more relevant to your recovery. By knowing these important aspects, treatment becomes simpler and more effective.

In Jane's case it is important to realize that her symptoms of anxiety and depression are a result of her unique response to an abusive father and unstable home environment. Jane is different from any other person, so the way she responds to stress, diet, or environmental influences is different from how other people would react in similar circumstances. It is also vital to understand that other people with similar emotions to Jane might have a different cause to their emotions and need a different approach to their treatment.

For example, another patient of mine, Tina, thirty-three years old, had suffered from anxiety and depression since she was a child. No matter how much counseling she tried, she did not get better. We finally found out that she always got anxious and depressed after eating wheat. Her digestive system was intolerant to gluten, a substance found in wheat and other grains. The chemical reactions to gluten in her body were altering her brain chemistry, leading to her depression. After removing wheat from her diet, she recovered completely!

Symptoms of Depression and Anxiety

A person is diagnosed with depression typically when they have five of the symptoms below most of the time, persisting for longer than two weeks, and if these symptoms interfere with their social or work life. I believe many of us suffer with some of these symptoms enough to warrant healing, even though we might not be diagnosed with a mental illness.

- Excessive feelings of guilt, hopelessness, despair, and/or worthlessness.

- Difficulty concentrating or difficulty making decisions.

- Sleep disturbances—either insomnia or oversleeping.

- Unnecessary or chronic irritability.

- Avoiding social situations and activities or withdrawal from people .

- Fatigue or feeling tired often for no apparent reason.

- Lack of motivation, interest, or pleasure in activities they used to enjoy.

- Weeping frequently for no apparent reason, feeling sad all the time, gaining no pleasure from anything.

- Loss of or increased appetite or weight.

- Frequent thoughts of suicide.

Typical signs of anxiety include:

- Panic, restlessness, hyper-arousal, fear, paranoia, and intrusive or unwanted thoughts.

- Uncertainty, apprehension, indecision, hopelessness, or feeling paralyzed.

- Constant worry, tension, anxiousness, or uneasy feelings that have no definite explanation.

- Inability to feel confident about managing simple situations.

Sometimes depression and anxiety may manifest with physical signs, such as:

- Loose bowel movements, diarrhea, stomach cramps, or nausea.

- Difficult or shallow breathing, tightness in the chest, heart palpitations, feelings of faintness, dizziness, dry mouth, or sweaty hands.

- Muscle pains, jaw tightness, grinding teeth at night or during the day, lack of sleep, or chronic fatigue.

Different situations that might cause anxiety in people include:

- Being in social gatherings.

- When a person is left alone and is uncomfortable being alone.

- When blood-sugar levels drop too low, due to physiological problems such as hypoglycemic episodes.

- When someone is confronted with their phobias; for example, failing an exam, meeting people, seeing a dog, or being exposed to heights.

- When someone is reminded of a traumatic experience that has not been fully resolved. This is most often seen in post-traumatic stress disorder (PTSD).

Different people respond differently to similar situations, which is why each person needs to be treated uniquely and individually. The way a person manifests his or her symptoms, be it anxiety, depression, or paranoia, depends on their unique characteristics, including genetics, diet, and physical and emotional makeup. A person's living conditions, work and social stress levels, support systems from people and community programs, socioeconomic status, and other factors also affect their ability to cope with stress and affect the way their emotions develop.

MENTAL EXERCISES TO IMPROVE WELLBEING & HEAL THE PAST

"A man too busy to take care of his health is like a mechanic
too busy to take care of his tools."
~ Spanish Proverb

A PRIMAL PART OF your brain, known as your limbic brain, is designed to protect you through instinctive survival mechanisms. Your limbic brain reacts automatically to situations based on previous stressful experiences you have had, and it can **continue to behave** in a defensive mode even though the initial threatening experience may no longer be present in your life. If a traumatic or stressful experience is not fully resolved, your brain will unconsciously continue to send stressful signals to your body, especially your adrenal glands. These signals put unnecessary and prolonged stress on your body, inevitably leading to adrenal fatigue, disease and emotional problems.

Online consultations, training, group healing seminars and healing journey safaris available
from www.drameet.com

Psychotherapy, emotional freedom technique, homeopathic medicines, and other therapies that I describe below help free your brain from its unconscious stressed state and return it to its relaxed or neutral state, which also stops the stress your mind puts on your adrenal glands. Healing stressful emotional memories actually **changes unhealthy neural connections** in your brain into healthier connections, using neuroplasticity, which is the ability of your brain to rewire its nerve connections. Such changes actually alter the emotional interpretations you have of old stressful memories, allowing you to have more positive emotions and a longer lasting healthier perspective on life.

The exercises in this chapter help your brain resolve stressful situations from your past. They allow your brain to replace negative or stressful emotions with healthier emotions and thought patterns using neuroplasticity. This leaves you less traumatized and less stressed than before. As you do these exercises, remember to reduce inflammation and heal your body as well, as I have described in Part 2 of this book. **Inflammation and unbalanced hormones** (please see Part 2) actually **reduce the ability of your brain to make healthier nerve connections**, making it difficult to feel emotionally well even if you try and remain positive through these exercises.

Daily practice of these exercises will reduce your predisposition to stress, anxiety, depression, and negative thoughts. Your mind will begin to feel safe. When your mind feels safe, you begin to relax and become more open to happier feelings feels more ready to do so. Having a positive and relaxed mind also helps you to expect more positive experiences in your life, which changes the way you approach life and brings better things to you. Your overall happiness will therefore be more a result of the **internal healing** of your own perceptions and emotions, rather than changes of external circumstances in your life.

Each of these exercises can be done separately or together, and some can be done every day. I highly suggest doing each and every exercise and doing the daily ones regularly. Make sure you actually each exercise after reading it rather than going through them in your mind. You have to fully engage in these exercises in order for your mind to experience their complete benefit.

Developing Emotional Resilience

The following exercises are things you can do daily to develop a positive mindset and better emotional resilience. Use them regularly, especially when you are going through difficult times, and watch out for change!

What Went Well the Previous Day

Research shows that remembering and writing down what went well for you during the day the increases your happiness for longer periods of time. I always do this exercise in the mornings in bed, especially when I used to wake up with that awful sense of dread, despair, and gloom. Remembering and writing down positive experiences helps your brain to better acknowledge that positive experiences are truly a part of your life and that not much has to change in your life for you to feel good every day. Writing and focusing on positive experiences every day also breaks your pattern of experiencing negative thoughts and beliefs, and you will eventually realize that you can feel good most of the time.

At the end of the day and every morning when you wake up, mentally go through or write down what you accomplished or what went well for you during the day and the previous day. It could be finishing a task, managing to exercise, going out with a friend, having a laugh, or even receiving a smile from someone. Make sure you acknowledge at least eight circumstances that went well for you or that made you happy. Try it now. Spend 20 minutes writing down everything that went well or did not go wrong for you for the past 2 days. I've left some space for you here to do this:

Giving Yourself Permission to Heal

A lot of our emotional issues actually come from an unconscious re-sistance we have to allowing ourselves to accept a better way of being. Many of us are also **unwilling to let go** of certain ideas or emotions we have become used to. You might not even be aware of these subtle resistances which hold you back from feeling better. I have created an exercise which allows you to overcome some of these unconscious resistances. I used this exercise successfully when working with victims of the Kenya Westgate terrorist attack, and, even after such a traumatic experience, I saw people's anxiety peel away, their breath-ing change, and their trauma and tension turn to a sigh and smile of relief. It's a very powerful exercise if done right.

I'd like you to start a daily exercise where you say to yourself: "it's safe to (...be happy, feel this way, let go, heal, feel strong, be in love, etc...)" or "it's okay to ..." and feel what happens inside of you as some of your limiting thoughts begin to surface. This is a powerful exercise you can do whenever you feel any emotional discomfort. I've used it many times and am always surprised to discover what thoughts have been holding me back without me even knowing it.

Whenever you try this exercise, search inside yourself for what you'd like to feel or what you're struggling with, and say "It's safe to..." Add the word "sometimes" or "once in a while" after your sentence. This helps your mind accept your sentences much more easily.

Even if you feel something negative and you don't know what belief is holding you back, try saying "It's safe to feel this way and recover" – you'll suddenly give yourself permission to let go of your internal struggle and feel a sense of relief and internal strength. I'm listing a few sentences to help you on your way. Notice how you feel after saying each of these sentences. If you feel any resistance or emotion coming up, accept these feelings and allow them to change as you meditate deeper on your positive intention.

"It's safe (okay) to feel okay sometimes."
"It's safe (okay) to be happy again."
"It's safe (okay) to be rich and successful sometimes."
"It's safe (okay) to be okay with these feelings sometimes."
"It's safe (okay) to be in love again or to love someone again sometimes."
"It's safe (okay) to be in power again."
"It's safe (okay) to feel love for myself again once in a while."
"It's safe (okay) to feel this way sometimes."
"It's safe (okay) to smile to myself again once in a while."
"It's safe to feel important again, once in a while."
"It's safe to love myself again, once in a while."

Being Grateful

I used to struggle with what *being grateful* means. I thought I was being grateful because I wasn't really criticizing anything in life. I thought that in the back of my mind I must already be grateful. However, after a few awakenings of realization in my life, I began to realize that being grateful is about fully and actively appreciating specific feelings and details about people, things or events. Being grateful involves a full hearted acknowledgment rather than something you think you already do in the back of your mind. Being grateful does not take away precious time from important things in life but actually gives you back important time to feel what's really precious in your life.

Being grateful is a powerful way to improve your emotional wellbeing. Studies show that people who practice gratitude are **less**

Online consultations, training, group healing seminars and healing journey safaris available from www.drameet.com

stressed and less depressed. If you ever wake up in the morning with anxiety or a sense of dread, spend some moments feeling gratitude for as much as you can, and go through everything that went well for you, didn't go wrong or made you smile or relax the previous day. Every day write down ten things you are grateful for. When you wake up in the morning, say thank you for this wonderful day, and say thank you for at least five things you are or can be grateful for. Search your mind for people you could have thanked. If someone has been kind to you in the past, thank them verbally or in your mind if you cannot get a hold of them, even if it has been a while since you saw them last.

Instead of thinking about what is not going well in your life or what you still haven't accomplished, think about how much you wanted some of things you now have and acknowledge that they are now in your life, and appreciate it. Even in the most difficult circumstances, where nothing beneficial is apparent, find something you can be grateful for, even if it unrelated to the difficult situation. Searching for positive aspects of difficult situations **transforms the way you respond to life** and gives you the courage to be more proactive and create more positive changes for yourself. Practicing this regularly every day will infuse your mind with positive thoughts and emotions so you are less likely to lapse into negative feelings.

Make a **commitment** to yourself **for the next 7 days** to only imagine what is going well or what went well, doing this throughout the day for 7 days, no matter what is going on. If you're stressed or there's a stressful situation, pause for a moment, and divert your mind to think about what you are grateful for or what went well the previous day, or what has been going well for you in your life. It could be simple things like "I have a bed to sleep on", "I'm earning some money", "I'm grateful for my breath", or "I have a family or people who care about me". Over time your mind will automatically have more positive thoughts to think about, and will move away from stressful thoughts and painful emotions. Go ahead now and write about 10 things you can be grateful for in the space I've left for you:

Setting Positive Intentions

"To wish to be well is a part of becoming well."
~ Seneca

Sometimes when we want change in our life, we focus too much on the negative thing we want to get rid of. Instead, talk about what you want in a positive way. State what you want, which gives your mind and heart a clear intention to work on, rather than saying what you want to get rid of, which is more complaining about your situation and reinforcing your negative thoughts and feelings. For example, rather than say, "I want to get rid of my sadness and depression," say words like, "I want to feel happier in my life." The second sentence increases the feeling of what you want in you, and it makes you more aware of the steps involved to get you to where you want to be. It also makes you aware of **certain feelings or ideas** that you have and were **not willing to give up on**. This clarity increases your ability to take the necessary steps to bring positive changes into your life. Write at least ten positive change sentences for yourself, and read them out loud at least once a day or whenever you're feeling gloomy.

Online consultations, training, group healing seminars and healing journey safaris available from www.drameet.com

Here are some positive change sentences that will help you get started:

- I want to feel calmer in my life (rather than saying, "I want to feel less anxious.")

- I want to smile more often.

- I want to have more positive thoughts

- I want to be and feel happy.

- I want to laugh more.

- I want to be in a relationship that is happy and good for me.

- I want to be in a place where I feel free and happy.

- I want to have positive thoughts about the future.

- I want to feel refreshed in the morning.

- I want to feel financially free.

- I want to be happier with myself, I want to think about myself and smile.

- I want to feel confident in myself.

- I want to heal from this.

Be specific about your goals and desires. Go ahead and write some down. Push yourself, explore, enjoy, and really feel the things you want! In the beginning, it might be difficult to pin down precisely what you want; however, as you do this process, a sense of clarity will emerge, and it will be easier to imagine what truly makes you feel better. After a while, you will automatically begin to let go of sadness, despair, and other negative thought patterns, and you will be able to focus more on positive thoughts and emotions.

Effective Meditations

"Nature, time and patience are three great physicians."
—H. G. Bohn

There was a time in my life when I was extremely stressed, confused and indecisive and had no sense of what I truly wanted for myself. I went to different therapists, and they all helped a bit, but nothing stopped the confusion or gave me a sense of peace until I started to meditate. As simple as it sounds, it was one of the most powerful gifts I gave myself. It helped me connect to an inner truth that really felt like my own, and this gave me so much power remain calm, make my own decisions and understand what I really wanted for myself.

Most people have their own specific way of meditating; however, some people find it quite difficult to meditate. I have described a few simple techniques for you below. Instead of trying to meditate for a long time at one sitting, it is actually more therapeutic to do **shorter meditations frequently during the day**, even for only five minutes at a time. Meditation helps you to develop more positive thoughts and make more rational decisions for yourself. Daily meditation improves neurotransmitter levels in your brain, reduces anxiety, lifts your mood, helps to resolve deeper emotional issues, and connects you to your higher spiritual self.

A simple meditation

- Sit in a comfortable position either on a cushion on the floor, or on a chair, with your back straight and the backs of your palms resting on your thighs.

- Touch the tips of your thumbs to your index fingers. Close your eyes softly, and shift your mind's focus to your breathing, allowing your breath to follow its natural rhythm.

- Imagine that your breath is made of white light and love, and all this light and love is **permeating every cell** of your body and healing every part of you wherever it goes, including your thoughts and emotions.

- Meditate in a calm, clean, and uncluttered environment, preferably close to some plants or out in nature. Share your healing light and love with the plants around you and imagine the plants sharing their healing light and love with you. This increases the amount of positive energy you receive from the environment.

- Meditate for at least two minutes whenever you have a chance during the day, and then slowly work your way up to ten minutes or longer.

- If your mind becomes crowded with thoughts during your meditation, observe these thoughts without trying to fight them away and without judging them. As you observe these thoughts, observe what reactions they evoke in you, and allow those reactions to occur without struggling against them. Let these thoughts disappear gently as you return to your visualization. Allowing your thoughts and feelings to come and go during your meditation develops harmony and patience in your mind and helps you become more comfortable and confident in yourself. As you become more comfortable with your feelings, your thoughts will have less power to create stress in your body.

- Other forms of meditation, apart from focusing on your breath, include visualizing different images, such as golden light in the center of your forehead, a peaceful candle flame, the ocean, the sky, or nature.

Another way to meditate is to visualize words like *joy, love, forgiveness, and peace.* **Smiling and meditating on positive words** can be very uplifting. Close your eyes and imagine the word *joy*, and let your feelings follow the idea of joy. Smile when you remember to smile and relax in the sensation of joy.

Meditating daily creates harmony in your heart, and you will feel less disturbed by stressful situations. Positivity will come more naturally to you, and you will begin to feel more comfortable with yourself.

Forgiveness, Disappointments and Expectations

Forgiveness can be a difficult thing sometimes. Most of us, even when we try to forgive, are still left with a feeling of hurt or disappointment. This is normal. Even though you know it might be good for you to forgive someone or something, your mind might not be ready to let go or forget. In fact, sometimes saying *"I forgive you"* to someone still leaves you with a feeling that something wrong happened between you and that the person might still be guilty.

Through my training in family constellations therapy, I found a new humble and more complete way of saying "I forgive you". It's by saying "I'm sorry this happened for me with you", or "I'm sorry this happened for us", or "I'm sorry this happened for me with us", or a similar version to this. Saying it this way allows you to accept and let go of the situation more completely and peacefully. It also removes any blame you still hold for the person and doesn't leave you with a false sense of superiority. Try it out. Even if you don't feel like forgiving someone who hurt you or disappointed you, try saying this, either to them directly or in your mind, and see what happens. Forgiveness sets your mind free of negative energy, thoughts and blame. It allows you to move forward more peacefully and positively.

Resentment and disappointment torment your mind, make you more negative and prevent you from living life positively. Similarly, unmet expectations can be a great source of unconscious depressive energy that we carry around with us. According to some therapists, unmet expectations and disappointments, especially related to our parents, can be a source of chronic depression without us knowing it. Think about all the unmet expectations or disappointments you have experienced with people. Whether you expected them to do something for you, or if they behaved in a certain way, or if they took something from you – whatever it is, do a mental check and see if you have any anger, resentment, disappointment or sad feelings around any memories. Now, really let go of these expectations and disappointments, and say the *forgiveness sentence* "*I'm sorry this happened...*" to all of these memories. Really make a mental effort to pull away from this stagnant energy which is holding you back from living life and smiling to yourself often enough. Say "It's safe to let go", or "It's safe to feel this way", or "It's safe to feel forgiveness sometimes", or any other sentence will free you from the grip of resentment and disappointment. Once you can move away from these feelings, your brain will rewire itself, and you will free up some mental space for more positive thoughts and feelings.

Emotional Freedom Technique

Developed by Gary Craig, Emotional Freedom Technique (EFT) is one of the fastest-growing methods people are using to find relief from emotional problems. In EFT, you **say statements** about your feelings and **tap on particular acupuncture points** on your body. Even though EFT may seem bizarre to do at first, EFT brings significant emotional relief immediately and changes negative beliefs and perceptions into more positive experiences.

- To perform EFT, choose an emotion or experience you are struggling with and that you want to change into a more positive one.

- Using your right fingertips, tap on the fleshy part of the edge of your left palm below your little finger (known as the "karate chop point") while saying the following phrase three times: "Even though I... (Say your issue here, e.g., "am hurt by my partner's arrogance toward me" or "am feeling really depressed right now"), I deeply and completely love and accept and respect myself."

- Shorten your starting sentence into a summary sentence (for example, the above sentence can become, "hurt by Steven's arrogance"), and tap at least three times on the following points on your body while saying the shortened version of your sentence:

1.   *On the bone near the inner corner of your eyebrow (left or right eye, it doesn't matter)*

2.   *On the bone on the outer edge of your eye*

3.   *On the bone underneath your eye*

4.   *On the flesh above your lip and underneath your nose*

5.   *On the flesh above your chin and beneath your lower lip*

6.   *On the inner part of your collar bone*

7.   *On your fourth rib underneath your breast*

8.   *On the side of your ribs underneath your armpit*

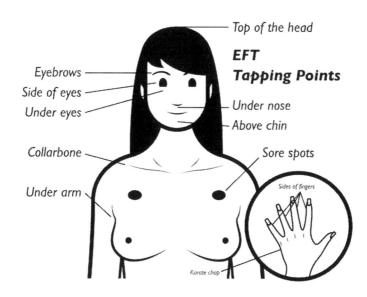

You might feel a shift in awareness about your feelings, and you can **alter your sentence to match your new feelings**. For example, you might say "less depressed" or "feeling relieved" while you continue to tap. Once you reach the end tapping point underneath your armpit, start again if you still have any negative feelings left. Change your sentence to closely match any new feelings you are experiencing. This is a simplified version of EFT and more details and more precise tapping points can be found on the internet, including free manuals on EFT. The beauty of EFT is that it uses acupuncture points as well as positive affirmations to create new neural connections in your brain, and it discharges emotional holding patterns, creating long-term benefits very easily.

Healing Rumination

"Sometimes your joy is the source of your smile, but sometimes your smile can be the source of your joy."
—Thich Nhat Hanh

Rumination happens when you spend time thinking negatively about your issues, self-reflect negatively, focus on feelings associated with negative situations in your life, or think about how you might have done things differently. Rumination often involves other thoughts such as fear, worry, regret, guilt, and shame, which are **not solution-oriented or forward-moving**. Rumination stresses your brain and makes anxiety and depression worse, and it also keeps you from engaging in healthier thoughts, conversations, relationships, and activities that would avoid negative feelings. The sad thing is that stressed, anxious, tired, and depressed people find it harder than others to stop rumination and turn their thoughts into more positive ones, making this a vicious cycle.

Rumination happens when your mind has not or cannot fully resolve a difficult emotional experience. Counseling, especially psychotherapy, reduces rumination by helping you come to terms with emotional experiences. By sharing your feelings with a therapist and releasing difficult emotions, your brain creates **new**

neural connections that are **less emotionally charged.** . This healing allows you to feel happier and have healthier thoughts.

Rumination is sometimes hard to overcome because it involves thought processes that are trying to solve important issues in your life. Even if you want to stop, you might feel anxious about letting go of rumination because it means you will leave your problem unsolved and leave yourself vulnerable to the difficult situation. Feeling comfortable enough to let go of rumination and focus on other pleasant things will come with practice.

If counseling is not an option for you, there is another way to beat rumination. First, you need to recognize that rumination increases mental stress and depression and does not solve much. Second, think about the things you typically ruminate on and identify situations or times when you usually ruminate (like driving to work, sitting alone at home in the evenings, etc.). Catch yourself ruminating every time it happens, and **find a distraction** as soon as possible. Here are a few ways you can break the rumination cycle.

- Phone a friend, listen to some music, play with your pet, or go shopping and engage in conversations with the shop's staff or even with a stranger. If you can, share your feelings with a friend because it helps to get a different perspective on your problems and possible solutions.

- Do all the other exercises described in this chapter. Paint a picture or journal about your thoughts by writing continuously about them for five minutes straight without taking your pen off the paper. Free writing in this way releases emotions and creates healthier neural pathways in your brain. By resetting neural pathways, your brain loses some of its tendency to ruminate on the same memories because you have changed the emotional context of the memories through the emotional discharge.

- Start saying positive affirmations all the time. Positive affirmations break the cycle of negative thought patterns and also help you to begin believing that you can feel okay. Once you begin believing in more positive possibilities, your mind becomes more motivated and you end up feeling better more often. Say things to yourself like: "I'm happy, lucky, strong and blessed"; "good things happen to me every day"; "life is getting better and better for me everyday"; "I feel good inside"; "It's okay to feel this way"; "I love you (to yourself in the mirror)"; "You're important (to yourself in the mirror)"; "sometimes these things happen and it's okay"; "it's okay to forgive myself sometimes". Even if you cannot believe or feel the essence of these sentences at the moment, continue saying them because by focusing on positive affirmations instead of negative ruminating thoughts, your brain actually feels less stressed and slowly begins to rewire itself towards better health.

- Do a quick set of sit-ups or push-ups; jog on the spot; clean the dishes; write down what you need to do for the week; go for a quick walk; or meditate on positive thoughts such as love, peace, and joy. I find exercise to be one of the best ways to break rumination, especially when I'm exercising with somebody else. Having company, even if you don't talk to each other, helps you engage with someone else rather than being preoccupied and isolated with your own thoughts.

- I avoid eating alone as much as possible. Eating alone can be extremely depressing. If you have to be alone while eating, listen to music or practice being grateful for every little thing in your life, including every bite of food. Studies show being grateful consistently minimizes the progression of depression. When I was visiting India, a hotel actually had a goldfish swimming in a bowl on every table occupied by single people.

- Do anything that is not thinking negatively about your issues, even if it means painting, smiling at the clouds, talking to a tree, or laughing at yourself.

Completing Small Tasks

Too often in depression we leave our life in shambles and allow unfinished activities to fester. A depressed person is not motivated to do much. The unfinished tasks linger in our minds and use up a lot of unconscious energy. We **lose energy this way**, and procrastination becomes both a habit and a struggle. The problem is, the more tasks you leave unfinished, the more overwhelming your life seems to be, discouraging you more from trying to accomplish anything and depressing you even further.

By accomplishing small tasks such as cleaning your bedroom, paying a bill, writing one email, or taking your dog for a walk, your mind actually **feels a sense of accomplishment**, satisfaction, and pleasure. Frequent experiences of accomplishment, pleasure, and satisfaction strengthen your sense of confidence and motivation, enabling you to do other tasks more easily. If you're feeling stuck, just trust that you have to complete one small task, and no matter how unmotivated you feel about it, commit yourself to completing it. Remember, it could be as small as mailing a letter, cleaning your room, paying a bill, writing your goals for the week (a really good activity), or calling someone you love. Once you start feeling the satisfaction of small accomplishments and recognize procrastination as the avoidance of risking change, you will feel motivated to do more for your life. Just start with one task at a time, right now!

Healing the Past

The next set of exercises help to release old and existing trauma from your mind so that you can free up your mind to become more present and enjoy life more fully. Try not to re-traumatize yourself when you think of some of your old memories – be gentle with yourself and seek professional help if some of these memories are too difficult to deal with on your own.

Timeline Release Healing Diary

Sometimes getting an overall perspective of our experiences in life helps to heal a lot of our beliefs and feelings. In this exercise, I'd like you to draw a timeline chart of your life, beginning from birth till your present life. You can use the chart I've drawn for you. On the left side, according to time, list all the physical experiences that had a significant impact on you. On the right side, list all the emotional experiences you have had in your life that either made you feel ashamed, traumatized, stressed, guilty, fearful, or unwanted, or created any other feeling that was uncomfortable. Even if you feel these experiences are irrelevant for you today, write them down still, because when they occurred, they did have an impact on you, however small.

Now, starting with the most recent emotional experience, write continuously about anything that comes to mind surrounding your experience. **Write for fifteen minutes** without taking your pen off the paper. Continue writing even if what you're writing doesn't make sense. This exercise helps you to **release trapped emotions** connected to your experiences and helps you to see your life more clearly and calmly. Do this for a maximum of two past experiences per day, not more, since you will not fully resolve the experiences if you crowd your mind with a lot of emotional processing.

You might need to repeat this exercise for certain events that take longer to resolve. Take your time in this healing journey. Be patient with yourself. Do not judge what you write on paper. Just continue writing over the next few weeks or months and notice how much better you feel as you get a renewed and more empowered perspective over your life.

Physical Events   Emotional Events

Birth

Present Day

Relaxed Breath in Past Memories

This is an exercise I created and find that it works really well. If you have any memory that is stressful or negative, I invite you to reconnect with that memory in your mind. As you imagine yourself in that situation, notice how you are breathing. Begin calming your breath down, breathing in a relaxed way as you still focus on the memory. Allow your mind and emotions to shift as you continue to calm your breath down. Trust in the process and accept whatever changes are happening. Use this exercise on every experience you have written down in your timeline healing diary and notice how different you feel. Even though this seems like a very simple exercise, I find it very useful in helping our brain reorganize some of the disturbing memories that we carry.

Changing Your Story

In life, we often create a story for ourselves. For example, you might say things like, "I haven't recovered since my girlfriend broke up with me," or "I feel victimized by what happened, and it wasn't fair," or "I was too shy as a kid so I never made enough friends at school," or some other story that you keep identifying yourself with. If you identify yourself with what I call victimized or powerless stories, **you continuously behave as if these stories still have an effect on you**, and it becomes difficult to create healthier and more functional behaviors until you begin to change your story of yourself.

If you **retell your story** to yourself and to others in a different way, still keeping it truthful, you give your brain a chance to adjust and to feel a sense of power over the situation rather than feeling victimized. I tell you, this is one of the most powerful and life-changing exercises I have experienced.

For example, a small story from my childhood could be retold in the following way:

> My teacher walked up to me one day in the classroom and was very cross that I had my lunch box next to my desk. I

had no idea that this was a problem. She picked it up and flung it across the floor to the other end of the classroom and screamed at me. I felt extreme shame and terror and have been afraid of her ever since.

I can slow down the events in my memory into different pieces, making it easier for my brain to process small parts of the story in little steps:

> I was sitting by my desk when suddenly my teacher walked up to my desk and was angry at me for something. I am not quite sure what. In her anger, she picked up my lunch box and threw it across the floor. I was ashamed and confused, and I think it was because my lunch box was next to me, even though I am still not sure if this was the real problem.

Since I have separated different parts of the experience into separate emotional components, I can see clearly that perhaps the teacher was not only angry with me, but just an angry person. I can even try a little humor in my story to make it lighter for me:

> My teacher was a really strict and angry woman, and all the kids were afraid of her. She even came up to me one day and threw my lunch box across the floor of the classroom and screamed at me. I was shocked, and all the kids were surprised, but we knew that was her typical behavior.

In retelling the story this time, I realize that a lot of kids were afraid of her and that maybe she was a generally angry woman. I give myself a chance to feel less guilt and shame about the whole situation because all the kids were afraid of her, and her anger was not only personalized toward me. I suddenly feel a sense of support from all the kids in the classroom. Perhaps my teacher did not know how to behave appropriately with children and was emotionally irresponsible. As I realize the generality of my teacher's anger, I feel a slight shift in my body where I was holding onto some fear from my past, and I now feel less threatened by the memory of her.

It might take many attempts for you to feel less emotionally affected by your story. This is OK. Every time you feel a slight shift in awareness or feeling, your brain is recovering from the event. You can also write your story out differently many times and go through the awareness shifts on your own; however, it's better to do it with people because of the energetic exchange you get from sharing with people. You can also do this as a group of about five or more people, with each person mingling with different people in the group, retelling their story in different ways with each person. Practice rewriting one of your memories below, a couple of times, and see if it makes a difference to you:

Imagining Positive Experiences

Another exercise to resolve emotional trauma from an event is to imagine the event occurring on a stage or on a television screen, with you as a spectator in the audience. As you watch the experience, imagine the event occurring slightly differently. Use your mind to bring in helping scenes or more positive outcomes to the event.

For example, to heal myself of a situation when I was emotionally abused by someone in my past, I imagine him on the screen looking away briefly from me and being interested in something else. This lessens the intensity of his glare and actually helps me breathe a little more deeply. As I continue the exercise over time, I might be ready to imagine this person walking away periodically. This gives me more breathing space and helps my brain reprocess the event in a more relaxed way. Doing this repeatedly actually rewires your brain and alters your emotions surrounding stressful memories, therefore stopping your brain from continuously stressing your adrenal glands.

Another memory I healed this way is when I found it difficult to recover from the intense grief I went through during a prolonged breakup with my girlfriend. It was a long period of rejections and arguments where I suffered quite a bit. What I did to lessen the intensity of my grief was to imagine her on the screen smiling at me once in a while during our hard times. Doing this reduced the pain in my mind that was still there and helped me smile a little, too. You see, I didn't need to change the entire memory—I altered it subtly enough so it remained believable in my mind. As I continued this exercise, I actually resolved a lot of grief and self-esteem issues that stemmed from this event and managed to develop a healthy relationship with someone else.

A third example is the memory of a teacher who was really mean to me when I was a child. As I envision him on the screen glaring and shouting at the *little me*, I imagine a bird coming to rest on his shoulder. Automatically, this discharges the focus in my brain from his anger and menacing look to something more gentle and safe to experience for a young child. I might even imagine my parents or somebody larger coming to talk to him as a way of protecting me. This also reduces the anxiety in my unconscious memory. Because I am less threatened and feel safer emotionally with my memory, my brain stops sending stressful unconscious signals to my adrenal glands, and I regain some of my emotional strength.

You might initially feel intense emotions doing these exercises. As you continue to do them, the intensity will lessen because your brain will have discharged some of the stress associated with your memories. Negative events in your past hinder your authenticity and alter the way you behave with others. If you continue to live your life in a compensated way, you perpetuate the negative feelings you carry inside of you. As you recover emotionally from past events, you begin to feel more confident and open in your life. Healing is an opportunity to awaken a freer and more joyful self and to interact with the world in a more positive and self-supportive way, which will hopefully bring you better health and more positive experiences.

Ho' oponopono

Ho'oponopono is an ancient Hawaiian practice of forgiving and loving the part inside of you that is experiencing a trauma or disturbing event. Ho'oponopono became famous when Dr. Ihale-akala Hew Len in Hawaii cured mentally ill criminals without even seeing them. He would study their medical charts and look within himself to find which part of his consciousness created the person's illness in his reality. As he forgave and loved this part inside him, Dr. Len managed to cure a whole ward of patients.

This seems like a farfetched story, however it has worked for many people and is based on the principles that everyone's world is a projection of what's inside of them and we are responsible for everything we experience in our world. We can heal anything by taking full personal responsibility for the experience and healing the part in us that is creating the experience. To do Ho'oponopono, whenever you feel disturbed by a situation or have a past trauma that is not fully healed, allow yourself to open up to the part inside of you which feels hurt or troubled by the experience, whether it's in the past or in the present. Once you feel this place inside of you, place both hands over your heart area in the center of your chest and say the following words to this stressed part of you with as much love and compassion as possible:

"I'm sorry, I love you, I forgive you, thank you."

You can think of these words silently, whisper them or say them out loud. Keep saying them to the stressed part inside of you, notice how you feel and trust the changes you are feeling inside. Do Ho'oponopono on each experience you wrote in your timeline healing diary to help lessen the emotions surrounding difficult situations in your life. I do Ho'oponopono on daily situations and on many past experiences and I often notice a shift in my emotions, in the way I relate to people and in the way I behave now.

Volunteering

Did you know that volunteering for a worthy cause actually improves emotional wellbeing? Yes, it's true. I've done it myself numerous times and it really feels good. Studies show that volunteering actually alleviates depression and prevents people from relapsing into depression as well. Volunteering also helps you develop social skills, gives you a chance to make contacts and friends, and prevents social isolation, which is a major cause and outcome of depression. Volunteering is often stress free and can feel rewarding, meaning your body will actually produce endorphins (feel good hormones) from feeling satisfied and appreciated. Give your time to a good cause this weekend, or whenever you have free time. Take a risk and find out what might be fun for you to do. You don't have to put yourself in a difficult situation to volunteer – I remember spending one weekend planting trees on Mount Kenya in the name of conservation. I'll give food to an orphanage for children with AIDS every Sunday, which is a really nice thing to do because the laughter and hugs from the children feels so good. These are just a couple of examples of nice environments where you can volunteer your time. And who knows, you might even help someone change their life for the better with a unique gift you didn't even realize you have!

Friends, Family, and Support Groups

"Friends are the medicine of life" - Unknown.

Being open with and gaining support from family, friends, and self-help groups can make a big difference if you suffer from emotional issues. It can be intimidating at first, but disclosing your problems to a trustworthy person starts a chain reaction of help and emotional release. They might give you advice, share a similar situation in their lives, or know someone who can help you. Even if you do not get all the help you need from the first person you talk to, sharing your problems with one person gives you the courage to open up and seek further help with other people.

As a friend or family member of someone with emotional issues, it is important to listen carefully when he or she discloses feelings and not be judgmental. Show that you care and are interested in the problems rather than immediately trying to suggest solutions. A person revealing anxieties and emotional issues is being vulnerable with you. The more you listen and allow that person to feel OK sharing this vulnerable side, the stronger and more open to help he or she will become.

Ask how you can be of help, but try to be patient and nonjudgmental if your help is refused. People with emotional difficulties often have a hard time judging the best solution. Another way you can help is to find meditation, yoga, personal-growth, or self-help groups. Perhaps you can attend a few sessions with the person to give some encouragement. Having support at the initial meeting or inquiry helps dissolve many barriers people experience when first seeking help.

Part 2

A BRIEF INTRODUCTION TO BRAIN CHEMICALS (NEUROTRANSMITTERS)

"Tears are often a sign of truth and not of weakness"
~ Dr. Ameet Aggarwal ND

BEFORE DISCUSSING THE physical contributors to emotional wellbeing, it is important to understand how chemicals known as neurotransmitters affect health. These chemicals, in your brain and throughout your body, have a strong impact on mental health. It is important to know that neurotransmitter levels are controlled by different organs and processes in your body, not only your brain

Dopamine is a neurotransmitter responsible for pleasure. It helps you feel relaxed, motivated, alert, and happy. If you feel **unmotivated, cannot concentrate, or crave coffee, chocolate, or other stimulants,** you're likely low in dopamine. Low levels of dopamine are also associated with incoherent thoughts, depression, and schizophrenia. Dopamine also controls physical processes, including digestion, heart and muscle control, and thyroid function. Nicotine in cigarettes increases dopamine production, which is why smoking, even though it's harmful to health, calms people down. Excessive dopamine in your body is harmful, though, because it suppresses serotonin, a neurotransmitter that improves your mood, keeps you calm, and is vital in preventing depression, anxiety, and other mood disorders. Because copper helps produce dopamine, copper toxicity, common in many people, causes an overproduction of dopamine, which reduces serotonin levels, leading to emotional problems.

GABA (gamma amino butyric acid) is a neurotransmitter that calms you down, improves sleep, and reduces stress, anxiety, panic attacks, and pain. If you feel **tense, have difficulty sleeping, and cannot relax**, your GABA levels are likely low, and you will also likely **crave sweet things or even alcohol** sometimes.

Serotonin is a key neurotransmitter that calms your nerves, reduces your stress response, helps you sleep better, gives you a sense of comfort, and increases your ability to feel pleasure. Serotonin is produced both in your brain and small intestine, which is why digestive health is so crucial to emotional well-being. When serotonin is low, your ability to feel pleasure decreases; you are likely more **negative, worried, or anxious**. You may have **trouble sleeping**; and be more prone to depression, obsessive-compulsive disorder, sleep disturbances, panic disorders, aggressive behavior, and suicidal tendencies. Low levels of serotonin also create **carbohydrate cravings**, which is why people with mood disorders often deal with cravings, binge eating, or other poor eating habits.

Norepinephrine is a neurotransmitter produced in your brain and by your adrenal glands. It keeps you alert and active, speeds up your breathing, constricts blood vessels, increases your heart rate, and increases your blood pressure. It is one of your *fight or flight neurotransmitters*, along with adrenaline. Norepinephrine levels should naturally decrease when alertness and important activities are not required. Very low levels, however, are linked with depression. When levels of norepinephrine remain elevated for a long time, or when they become over-elevated, people suffer from **insomnia** and tend to experience feelings of fear, panic, or anxiety. During panic attacks, when people experience a rapid heart rate and rapid breathing, it is usually norepinephrine and adrenaline that are elevated.

Online consultations, training, group healing seminars and healing journey safaris available from www.drameet.com

YOUR ADRENAL GLANDS AND EMOTIONAL WELLBEING

"Health is the greatest possession. Contentment is the greatest treasure. Confidence is the greatest friend. Non-being is the greatest joy."
~ Lao Tzu

NOW THAT YOU know more about neurotransmitters, you will understand how different organs in your body affect your mental health through their influence on neurotransmitters. Your adrenal glands are probably one of the most crucial organs to affect mental health. They are situated above your kidneys and help you cope with stress by producing chemicals such as cortisol, norepinephrine, and adrenaline.

During stressful periods, your adrenal glands go into overdrive and release their chemicals in large amounts, causing many physical symptoms. Your heart beats faster, your breathing increases, sugar is released into your blood for more energy, and blood flow increases to your muscles and brain to give them more oxygen and energy. This keeps your body and brain alert and ready for action. This state is also known as the **fight or flight** response, which humans and other animals developed as a primal response to threat and fear. This primal response still kicks in when we experience stress today.

"Sometimes stubbornness feels like strength. Underlying it though is a vulnerability that is often afraid of the unknown or it is your own fear of change... Allow yourself to be free and your strength will slowly come."

Adrenal Fatigue

Unfortunately, in today's world, we are under constant stress from work, phone calls, bills, deadlines, traffic, loud noises, computer vibrations, relationships, unresolved emotions, high cost of living, late nights, and other pressures of life. Your body does not distinguish this form of stress from the threat of an animal coming to eat you. It's all about survival. We never have a chance to switch off. Constant stress is unnatural for our bodies to experience, and it drives our adrenal glands into exhaustion.

Other issues also lead to adrenal burnout: poor diet, lack of exercise, long-term coffee use, high-sugar intake, poor stress management, environmental toxicity, and heavy metal toxicity (especially copper toxicity). Adrenal burnout, adrenal fatigue, or *hypoadrenia*, is now one of the most common ailments in society today and is likely a leading cause of most chronic health problems, including anxiety, depression, chronic fatigue, poor immunity, heart disease, insomnia, low sexual performance and interest, and thyroid problems.

With adrenal stress, your body goes through various phases. The first two, called alarm and adaptation phase, are when cortisol, adrenaline, and noradrenalin are produced in large amounts continuously to cope with stress. With prolonged stress, your adrenal glands do not switch off, and high levels of **cortisol** are continuously produced. High amounts of cortisol suppress *feel-good hormones* such as dopamine, serotonin, and melatonin. This causes anxiety, increased fears, palpitations, lack of sleep, and a general sense of unease. It also causes blood sugar imbalances and cravings for carbohydrates (sugars), salt, and stimulants such as coffee.

The last phase, known as the exhaustion phase, is when your adrenal glands are completely burnt out and cannot regulate the production of hormones. Your levels of **hormones cycle improperly** during the day and night, spiking at times but being significantly low most of the time. This leads to depression, chronic fatigue, difficulty concentrating, insomnia, procrastination, low motivation, blood sugar imbalance, and chronic illnesses. During adrenal fatigue, your ability to cope with stress is significantly reduced. This means that the smallest amounts of stress, make you feel anxious or tearful and lead to other emotional reactions that you normally would not have in small stressful situations.

Your adrenal glands **regulate your blood sugar**, immune function, sex hormones, salt and electrolyte balance, and many other functions in your body. Adrenal fatigue is therefore also related to problems such as decreased immunity, high cholesterol, high blood pressure, frequent colds, hormonal imbalances, and other chronic diseases. Because of hormonal imbalances, it is not uncommon to see women with emotional issues also suffering from **irregular periods, painful sex, premenstrual syndrome, fibroids, ovarian cysts,** and other hormonally related conditions. The interconnectedness between your emotional well-being and physical body is evident yet again.

"Brian" was attacked by a lion while on safari in Kenya. A few years later, his business started going through some financial difficulties. The initial shock of the lion attack had stressed his adrenal glands, and the additional stress of his failing business pushed him further into adrenal exhaustion. Over the following years, even though his business recovered, Brian developed anxiety, insomnia, and mild depression. Even though he felt he had fully recovered from the scare of his lion attack and his business was picking up again, his anxiety did not disappear.

Because Brian's brain and adrenal system were still stuck in shock and stress from a few years ago, he was living his normal life with an unconsciously stressed mind and exhausted adrenal glands. Using homeopathic medicines and psychotherapy, we helped Brian resolve the traumatic experience and deal with stressful memories in a healthy way, so that both his body and mind calmed down and accepted he was safe now. We also put him on a B-complex multivitamin and adrenal-nourishing herbs to replenish his exhausted adrenal glands. Within six months, Brian was sleeping well again and was calm and confident, as much as he had been before all his troubles began.

Sugar, Caffeine, and Your Adrenal Glands

Eating high amounts of simple sugars and carbohydrates such as donuts, crackers, white bread, pastries, and sweets causes high surges of glucose in your blood. This forces your body to produce high amounts of **insulin** to remove the glucose from your blood and store it in your tissues as fat or in your liver as glycogen. When insulin levels surge, your adrenal glands are forced to make high amounts of hormones to bring your insulin levels back to normal. Putting too much sugar into your system literally raises the level of stress hormones in your body.

These continuous hormone surges exhaust your adrenal glands and create **unstable blood-sugar** levels, leading to less energy reaching your brain, which in turn causes foggy thinking, fatigue, poor concentration, anxiety, depression, irritability, and other mood disturbances. Eating proteins such as chicken, fish, nuts, seeds, or tofu, which are digested much more slowly than simple carbohydrates, with all your meals, ensures a steady and slow release of nutrients into your bloodstream. This minimizes insulin and cortisol spikes and prevents adrenal fatigue. **Nutrition affects hormones, and hormones affect emotions. It really is that simple.**

Sugars and simple carbohydrates also lack essential healthy nutrients such as vitamin B5, vitamin B6, vitamin C, and zinc, which nourish your adrenal glands. Therefore, eating these foods provides no nourishment to your adrenal glands but merely pushes and exhausts them. Similarly with coffee, caffeine is a stimulant that pushes your adrenal glands to work harder without nourishing them with nutrients. Every time you eat and drink you have the opportunity to help stabilize blood sugar and hormone levels or wreak havoc with them.

Caffeine also interferes with your liver and causes inflammation in your digestive system. This leads to chronic diseases and emotional problems, as we will see in later chapters. Having decaffeinated coffee does not help because most decaffeinated coffee is made using unhealthy chemical processes. I often find that after removing coffee and replacing simple carbohydrates with more protein and green vegetables, many of my patients with anxiety and depression see remarkable improvement *in less than three weeks!*

Melatonin, Sleep, and Your Adrenal Glands

Melatonin is a hormone essential for sleep as it helps your body calm down. Melatonin levels naturally rise at night, and your body requires darkness to increase its production. Excessive cortisol reduces melatonin levels so **cortisol should decrease at night** in order to allow melatonin levels to increase. With adrenal stress, cortisol levels often remain high at night, preventing a sufficient rise in melatonin levels and interfering with sleep. Poor sleep patterns exacerbate anxiety and depression because your body never gets the rest it needs to recover from stress. As sleep patterns worsen, so does adrenal fatigue, which worsens sleep patterns, depression, and anxiety—a vicious cycle.

To ensure proper sleep, it is important to eat a good amount of protein for dinner. Simple carbohydrates get converted to glucose quickly and keep your brain very active late into the night. After a while, your blood-glucose levels fall rapidly, and your brain experiences starvation in the middle of the night, causing it to wake up to look for food. Eating protein prevents this because it is broken down more slowly and provides a slow and steady release of nutrients throughout your sleep. Think of your last meal of the day as 'feeding' a good night's sleep. More protein and less simple carbohydrates can make the difference between a calm, sleeping brain and a wakeful, hungry brain. Because **darkness is important for melatonin production**, make sure your room is completely dark when you go to bed, otherwise your levels of melatonin will be too low for deep sleep.

"Judy" was a patient with anxiety who had trouble sleeping. I could not figure out why until I just asked her, "Is your room dark enough?" We discovered that there actually was a street lamp outside her room, and her curtains were not thick enough to prevent the light pouring into her room. After she corrected this with thicker curtains, her sleep improved, and her anxiety reduced within two weeks. Melatonin is also used in preventing and treating some cancers, so having adequate amounts is truly beneficial to your overall health.

A Vicious Cycle with Nutrients

Nutrients such as **vitamin B5, vitamin B6, vitamin C, and zinc** are essential for adrenal gland health. These nutrients are also essential for the production of neurotransmitters and hormones in your body and the proper functioning of all your organs. Your adrenal glands use up a lot of these nutrients during chronic stress, causing a decline in neurotransmitter production, and a decline in your organs' ability to function well, taking a further toll on your emotional and physical health. Without adequate nutrition, your adrenal glands are no longer capable of coping with stress. Even normal experiences or small amounts of stress begin to feel overwhelming, and you are likely to experience anxiety more frequently.

"He who has health has hope, and he who has hope has everything".
—*Arabian Proverb*

Treating Your Adrenal Glands

Whenever I suspect someone has exhausted adrenal glands, I always start by helping them resolve any traumatic or stressful emotional experiences, either through psychotherapy or through energetic medicines such as homeopathy. Unresolved emotions, or **emotional holding patterns (EHPs)**, continuously stress your adrenal glands at an unconscious level and degrade emotional wellbeing, even if you take adrenal-nourishing herbs and nutritional supplements. Resolving traumatic or stressful experiences allows your adrenal glands to finally get a break from your unconsciously stressed mind.

Please refer to the chapter titled "The Effects of Emotional Experiences" to understand how unresolved emotions affect your adrenal glands. I have also described how to **release some unresolved emotional experiences** using mental exercises and energetic medicines in the chapters "Mental Exercises to Improve Wellbeing & Heal the Past" and "Homeopathy, Acupuncture, Counseling, Energy Medicine, Herbs and Nutrition."

Follow these healthy habits to preserve your adrenal glands and prevent further exhaustion:

- Avoid stressful lifestyle habits, coffee, high-sugar diets, recreational drugs, excessive alcohol, late nights, and stressful jobs, which all deplete your adrenal glands.

- Reduce inflammation and inflammatory foods in your diet (see chapter on "Your Digestive System") because inflammation in your body stresses your adrenal glands to make more cortisol in order to control the inflammation.

- Have a lot of fish oil supplements on a regular basis, since omega-3 fatty acids in fish oils reduce inflammation and also **improve brain function**. Remember, your brain is mostly made up of fat, and you need the good omega-3 type to repair and improve its function.

- Go to bed before or around ten o'clock at night, meaning *lights out!*

- Keep a regular routine. Your adrenal glands release specific hormones at specific times of the day, following a regular twenty-four-hour cycle. They are very sensitive to when you eat food, when you rest, when you exercise, and when you sleep. Keeping your work, exercise, and meal times regular ensures this regular cycle is maintained. Sporadic meal times and activities force your adrenal glands to work out of their natural rhythm and deplete them.

- Eat regular meals with larger amounts of proteins and green vegetables compared to smaller amounts of refined carbohydrates and sugars.

- Exercise, meditate, and do yoga and breathing exercises daily. **Regular exercise** is one of the most crucial cures for depression because it alters your brain chemicals more permanently than any drug out there. If you're too depressed to exercise, just stretch every part of your body whenever you can and go for brisk walks, a bike ride, or do sit-ups or jogging on the spot if you cannot leave the house. Just get moving, even if it's only for five minutes. Build up to ten minutes when the confidence comes, but just get moving.

- Use treatments like acupuncture, acupressure, reflexology, Bowen therapy (a profound body therapy developed in Australia), or massage, all of which help to discharge stress and improve health.

While you work on resolving emotions and follow healthy habits, you need to also nourish your adrenal glands back to optimal health using nutritional supplements and herbs. I have listed a few nutrients and herbs that nourish your adrenal glands below.

I also discuss other herbs, foods, and nutritional supplements for emotional well-being in the chapters "Herbal Medicines" and "Foods and Nutritional Supplements." If you want to know which foods the nutrients below are found in, please see the section on "Nutritional Supplements" later on in this book.

Food and Supplements That Heal Your Adrenal Glands

During stress, the amount of nutrients normally found in food is not enough to meet the demands of your adrenal glands and restore them back to health. Using nutritional supplements, which contain high amounts of nutrients, in addition to eating healthy foods is often necessary to cope with stress and ensure a more complete recovery.

Foods such as avocados, potatoes, bananas, chicken, peaches, cantaloupe, salmon, tuna, lima beans, and dried apricots nourish your adrenal glands.

Vitamins B1, B2, B5, B6, and B12 nourish your adrenal glands and should be used together. Vitamin B5, often called the *anti-stress vitamin*, is one of the best B vitamins for adrenal health. Stress, alcohol, excessive sugar consumption, and caffeine **deplete** your body of essential B vitamins. I have listed which foods contain different vitamins in the section on "Nutritional Supplements."

Vitamin C is crucial to nourishing your adrenal glands, improves your immunity, and reduces the damage caused by toxins in your body. Depending on the severity of your condition, vitamin C can be dosed higher than 1000 mg twice or thrice a day. Having too much vitamin C can cause loose stools, so check with your health practitioner how much you should be taking. Foods that have high amounts of vitamin C include: oranges, amla (Indian Gooseberry), grapefruit, kiwi fruit, lime, and berries.

Fats such as butter and fat from avocados, fish, and chicken are nourishing to your adrenal glands. Healthy oils such as coconut oil and omega-3 and omega-6 oils from fish, nuts, and seeds calm and rebuild your nervous system, reduce mental confusion, and improve mental clarity.

Melatonin, 5-HTP, Tryptophan, and Theanine are supplements commonly used to promote sleep. Melatonin is more effective when someone has trouble **falling asleep,** whereas 5-HTP and tryptophan are better to use when a person **wakes up** in the middle of the night and has interrupted sleep. Theanine, less effective than the other sleep supplements, is found in green tea and has a calming effect on the body and can help when you feel your sleep is not deep enough.

Phosphatidylserine is a fatty molecule that **reduces cortisol** levels in your body, giving a break to your adrenal glands. Phosphatidylserine can help reduce symptoms of anxiety and insomnia due to excessive cortisol while you use other supplements to restore adrenal gland health.

Zinc is one of the most essential nutrients for your adrenal glands and is at its highest concentration in your adrenal glands. Zinc strengthens your immune system, reduces fatigue, and has a calming effect on the body. Zinc also helps with **absorbing B vitamins** and helps produce various adrenal gland hormones. Low levels of zinc have been related to depression.

Herbs That Heal Your Adrenal Glands

Some of the herbs described in this book can be extremely dangerous if misused, if used for too long, if combined with other medications and other herbs, or if used during pregnancy or breast-feeding. Please consult a qualified practitioner before trying any of these herbs.

Herbal medicines can be used in a wide variety of ways when treating mood disorders, depending on what organ you want to treat. There are herbs that temporarily relieve anxiety or elevate your mood, and there are herbs that nourish your adrenal glands, cleanse your liver, or heal your digestive system. I recommend primarily using herbs that nourish your adrenal glands, cleanse your liver, and heal your digestive system because this approach often provides you with a longer-term cure.

Adrenal-nourishing herbs are considered **adaptogens**. Some adaptogens rejuvenate your adrenal glands more than others, and I've listed them below in order of what I believe to be their strength relative to one another. This order is not precise, since each herb has unique qualities that make it more suited for a specific condition.

Korean ginseng (Panax ginseng) is an adaptogen that strengthens and revitalizes your body and improves your body's resistance to long-term stress. Some ginsengs stimulate your adrenal glands; however, Korean ginseng is less stimulating and is a better ginseng to use for anxiety. Prolonged use of ginseng over-stimulates your body and misuse can worsen anxiety.

Rhodiola (Rhodiola rosea) nourishes your adrenal glands and re-stores the balance between your adrenal glands and your brain's **hypothalamus and pituitary gland**. Rhodiola is a deep-acting herb and provides long-term yet gentle strengthening for your adrenal glands. It is a great herb to lift you out of depression and alleviate anxiety that stems from stress and exhaustion, and it also increases your endurance during times of stress. Rhodiola is one of the best herbs to help restore neurotransmitter balance.

Liquorice (Glycyrrhiza glabra) is both nourishing and stimulating and supports your body during stress and helps build your im-munity. Liquorice is known to increase blood pressure and should not be used by anyone with high blood pressure.

Ashwagandha Root (Withania somnifera) strengthens your body and helps your adrenal glands to cope with and recover from stress. Ashwagandha is a great grounding and nourishing herb and is not too over-stimulating.

Astragalus Root (Astragalus membranaceus) is a tonic that helps your body resist the effects of stress and boosts your **immune**

system. It helps nourish and restore your adrenal glands without being too overstimulating.

Schizandra Berry (Schizandra chinensis) is a calming and adaptogenic herb. Popular in traditional Chinese medicine, it helps with depression, irritability, insomnia, and palpitations. Because it is a **sedative and a tonic** at the same time, Schizandra berry gives your adrenal glands a chance to recover by shutting off your body's stress response and nourishing your adrenal glands back to health without overstimulating them.

Bacopa (Brahmi, Bacopa monniera) is an herb used in Ayurvedic medicine with fantastic results. It is a gentle, **non-stimulating** adaptogen, making it excellent for anxiety and to reduce the effects of stress. It helps improve memory and learning abilities and is excellent for anxious and depressed people who are forgetful or have difficulty thinking clearly.

Borage (Borago officinalis) is a very **comforting**, adrenal-nourishing herb that helps with depression and anxiety. The beauty of Borage is that it also reduces the effects of stress on our adrenal glands. Borage **cannot be used during pregnancy**, so please be careful with it.

Holy Basil (Tulsi, Ocimum sanctum) has a very calming effect and lifts your mood at the same time. Tulsi helps clear your mind and is excellent to use when you have depression mixed with anxiety. Holy Basil leaves make a delicious, soothing tea.

Amla (Indian Gooseberry, Emblica officinalis) contains high amounts of vitamin C, even more than oranges do. **Vitamin C** is extremely important for adrenal gland health.

Oats (Avena sativa) are a very nourishing tonic for your nervous system and help build you up from exhaustion. Oats are especially soothing if you have nervousness due to exhaustion.

Testing Your Adrenal Glands

There are various laboratory tests you can do to assess the health of your adrenal glands. Note that even though some tests may show that your adrenal glands are healthy, you might still need to supplement with adrenal-supporting herbs or nutrients to stabilize your health.

Cortisol levels can be measured through your saliva, blood, or urine. Because cortisol levels cycle throughout the day, it is ideal to collect samples at four different times of the day to get an accurate picture of how your adrenal glands are functioning. Collecting a single sample of cortisol does not give an accurate picture of adrenal function. Ideally, the samples should be collected in the morning, at noon, in the evening, and at night. Salivary cortisol measurement is a popular test because it is easy to collect and gives an accurate indication of your cortisol levels at a specific time.

The **pituitary gland** in your brain releases a hormone called ***adrenocorticotropic hormone (ACTH)***, which stimulates your adrenal glands to produce cortisol. Laboratories can also measure blood levels of ACTH at different times during the day. This is one of the more accurate tests because it helps to see whether the problem is in your pituitary gland or in your adrenal glands.

The ACTH challenge test is used to see if your adrenal glands are responding well enough to ACTH. Laboratories will inject you with synthetic ACTH and measure how much cortisol your adrenal glands produce. If your adrenal glands do not produce enough cortisol after an ACTH injection, it is likely that they are not responding well to the ACTH from your pituitary gland.

The **urinary Koenisburg test** is conducted by mixing your urine with a chemical, and it measures the amount of chlorine in your urine and shows how much sodium your body is excreting. If your body is excreting excessive amounts of sodium, it is a sign of adrenal fatigue.

A quick test for adrenal health is to shine a flashlight into a person's eyes while they are in a dimly lit room. The **pupils of the eyes** will become smaller because of the bright light. With adrenal fatigue, the pupils will not be able to stay small for long and will quickly re-dilate slightly after becoming small.

YOUR DIGESTIVE SYSTEM AND EMOTIONAL WELL-BEING

"The doctor of the future will give no medication, but will interest his patients in the care of the human frame, diet and in the cause and prevention of disease."
~ Thomas A. Edison

I'VE NEVER TREATED anyone for anything without also addressing their digestive system and looking at their diet. Your digestive system is the seat of your health, and keeping it healthy prevents many chronic diseases. Your intestines have a lining that acts as a semi permeable barrier, controlling what is absorbed into your body from the food you eat. Numerous tiny blood vessels surround your intestines and absorb nutrients that pass through this **semi permeable barrier**, later transporting these nutrients to your entire body through your bloodstream. As you will see below, poor diet, antibiotic use, and lifestyle choices destroy the lining of your intestines, exposing your entire bloodstream to improperly digested food particles and toxins. These absorbed toxins and food particles cause unhealthy chemical reactions and inflammation throughout your body, compromising the health of every organ and altering your entire balance of hormones and brain chemicals.

Probiotics and Leaky Gut Syndrome

Your intestines have naturally occurring good bacteria known as **probiotics** that keep harmful bacteria and harmful yeast (also known as *Candida*) in your digestive system to a minimum. Probiotics also produce chemicals that protect the cell lining of your intestines. Antibiotic use, stress, improper diet, poor lifestyle, and other factors kill off your probiotics, allowing yeasts and harmful bacteria to increase in numbers. The harmful bacteria and yeasts release toxins in your intestines, which cause your intestinal cells to become inflamed and die off, leaving **gaps in your intestinal barrier**, a condition commonly known as *leaky gut syndrome*.

Leaky gut syndrome allows toxins and undigested food particles to enter your bloodstream instead of being filtered by your intestinal lining. These substances create a huge immune response because your body sees them as foreign and harmful to you. This immune response triggers **excessive inflammation** in your body, which produces more toxins and increased cortisol levels. It also alters the natural chemistry of your blood and tissues, causing chronic diseases and an imbalance of hormones and neurotransmitters, which, as we already know, leads to emotional problems.

The added toxicity from leaky gut syndrome also harms the health of organs such as your liver, pancreas, adrenal glands, and thyroid gland, all crucial to emotional stability. If your **liver** becomes burdened with toxins, its ability to clean your blood decreases, causing even more inflammation and toxins to build up in your body, and worsening the imbalance of cortisol, hormones, and neurotransmitters.

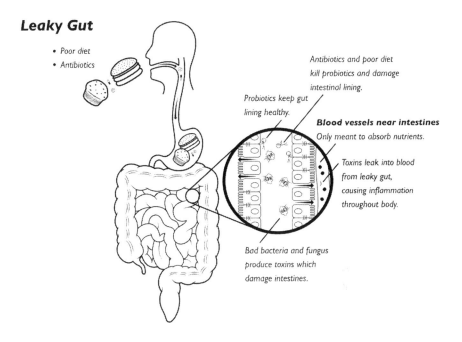

Leaky Gut

- Poor diet
- Antibiotics

Antibiotics and poor diet
kill probiotics and damage
intestinal lining.

Probiotics keep gut
lining healthy.

Blood vessels near intestines
Only meant to absorb nutrients.

Toxins leak into blood
from leaky gut,
causing inflammation
throughout body.

Bad bacteria and fungus
produce toxins which
damage intestines.

Your intestinal cells, pancreas, and liver are also responsible for producing digestive juices and enzymes to digest and absorb your food completely. If they become unhealthy, digestion and, therefore, **absorption of important nutrients** into your body is reduced. When nutrients aren't being absorbed properly, it affects your body's ability to produce brain neurotransmitters and enable optimal functioning, causing a decline in your mental and physical health.

Due to its contribution to chronic and excessive inflammation in your body, leaky gut syndrome also causes damage and **plaque** formation in your blood vessels, including those in your heart, kidneys, and genital organs, meaning increased risk of heart disease, kidney disease, poorer erections, and reduced sexual stimulation. Chronic inflammation is also a leading cause of skin issues such as eczema and psoriasis, increased food sensitivities, asthma, premenstrual syndrome, endometriosis, chronic sinusitis, arthritis, and other chronic diseases.

Treating Your Intestines

So how do we go about repairing your gut and reducing inflammation? It's fairly simple, and I'll show you how:

1. *Replenish the probiotics in your gut*

    High-strength probiotics are found in health- food stores (under different strains, such as *lactobacillus acidophilus, lactobacillus rhamnosus, saccharomyces boulardii, etc.*). Certain foods such as yogurt, fermented cabbage, and some raw vegetables also contain **probiotics** but not at therapeutic levels. Replenishing your probiotics to adequate amounts might take up to three months, so be patient with yourself. The effort is worth it, though, because you are building a strong foundation for long-term health.

2. *Increase your digestive enzymes and stomach- acid levels*

    Stomach acid (hydrochloric acid, or **HCL**) and **digestive enzymes** break food down properly so that your intestines better absorb nutrients. Stomach acid also helps kill harmful bacteria that might be in your food. Stress, improper eating habits, and digestive damage will sometimes cause levels of stomach acid and digestive enzymes to be lower than normal, even though most stressed people tend toward higher stomach-acid levels. Low stomach acid levels can also be due to low thyroid activity. Low stomach acid and low levels of enzymes allow poorly digested food and harmful bacteria to reach your lower intestines and cause further damage and inflammation, worsening leaky gut syndrome. Increasing stomach acid and digestive enzymes can be achieved using HCL capsules and digestive-enzyme supplements available through health-food stores. Use them with caution and under supervision because excessive stomach acid can damage your intestines.

3. *Improve your liver function*

Your liver produces bile, which helps break down fat and other foods. Impaired liver function leads to poor digestion and poor absorption of nutrients. I discuss how to heal your liver extensively in the section "Your Liver and Emotional Wellbeing."

4. *Reduce and correct the damage done to your intestines*

Removing inflammatory foods from your diet and eating healthy foods reduces damage to your probiotics and to your intestine. Inflammatory foods include coffee, sugar, refined grains (white bread, pastries, etc.), beef, and alcohol.

Some people are sensitive to foods called nightshades, which include aubergines (eggplant), tomatoes, and zucchinis, amongst others. You can get yourself tested for food allergies by a health practitioner. There are certain **hypoallergenic foods** that do not cause much inflammation and are safe to eat as part of an anti-inflammatory diet. See the list at the end of this section.

Omega-3 oils found in foods such as fish, nuts, and seeds also reduce inflammation in your body, unless you are allergic to these foods. Certain spices such as **cumin and turmeric**, used in Indian cuisines, also reduce inflammation and can be added to your cooking. Herbs such as liquorice and slippery elm are soothing and help heal your inflamed intestines. In addition to probiotics and healthy foods, I always use a nutritional supplement called L-glutamine. **L-glutamine** is an amino acid that provides a rich energy source to intestinal cells and helps to **heal your intestinal wall**. L-glutamine brings far better healing to your intestines than using probiotics alone. L-glutamine also helps make important brain chemicals, such as GABA, that reduce anxiety. Other nutrients that help to repair your intestines include **vitamin A, vitamin B5, folate, selenium, and zinc. Vitamin D and calcium** keep the environment in your intestines healthy for your different probiotics, so use these supplements while using probiotics.

More health benefits of these nutrients are discussed in the chapter on "Foods and Nutritional Supplements."

If you are on antibiotics frequently, it may be useful for you to discuss with your doctor how to reduce the amount of antibiotics you take because antibiotics destroy probiotics and reduce your immunity. Part of the reason children develop chronic infections is because they are given antibiotics too many times at an early age. It becomes a vicious cycle because the more antibiotics they take, the worse their immunity gets, and the sicker they get. Hence you see a lot of children with chronic infections or needing their tonsils removed. If you have used antibiotics in your life, you need to supplement with probiotics and other supplements and avoid inflammatory foods for several months. The good news is that once you repair your gut and remove inflammatory foods, you will have fewer infections because your immunity will improve. I recommend seeing a naturopathic doctor for a complete approach to healing your gut, building up your immunity, and addressing the root cause of your health problems.

5.   *Destroy harmful bacteria and yeast*

As you build up your intestinal health, it is time to kill off harmful bacteria and yeast. Killing off harmful bacteria and yeast can release a lot of toxins in your intestines due to the *die-off* reactions. Because of this, I prefer to improve intestinal health using the methods above for a couple of months before destroying bacteria and yeasts so as to prevent toxins from entering into your bloodstream.

Oregano oil and grapefruit seed extract are powerful herbs that act as antifungals. These two herbs are very strong and can be harmful in large amounts, so use them with caution. Herbs such as garlic, basil, olive oil, and coconut oil also have antifungal properties and can be added to your food on a regular basis.

Summary of Gut-Healing Nutrients and Foods

- Probiotics to replenish the good bacteria in your gut

- Vitamin D and Calcium to keep intestinal environment healthy for probiotics

- L-glutamine, vitamin A, vitamin B5, folate, selenium, and zinc to help heal your intestinal cell wall and reduce leaky gut syndrome

- HCL (stomach acid supplements), digestive enzymes, and liver herbs to increase digestion and absorption of food and to reduce harmful bacteria from reaching your lower intestines

- Turmeric (spice), nuts, seeds, and fish oils to reduce inflammation

- Liquorice (avoid in high blood pressure) and slippery elm to soothe inflamed tissues in your intestines

- Avoid inflammatory foods such as coffee, sugar, refined grains (white bread, pastries, etc.), beef, alcohol, and certain vegetables such as aubergine, tomatoes, and zucchini (nightshade vegetables)

- Oregano oil or grapefruit seed extract (both in very small amounts), garlic, basil, olive oil, and coconut oil to help kill any yeast or harmful bacteria

The Hypoallergenic Diet

The following list of foods was compiled at the Canadian College of Naturopathic Medicine (CCNM) and lists foods to eat and foods to avoid in order to minimize inflammation in your body. It is based on the work of many health practitioners, including naturopathic doctors, medical doctors, and nutritionists and has had tremendous health benefits for people suffering from all sorts of diseases. If you are ever in Toronto, I suggest visiting CCNM's Robert Schad Naturopathic Clinic, where teams of clinicians work together for you to optimize your well-being.

The hypoallergenic diet is divided into two stages. First, eliminate all allergenic foods for three weeks. If your symptoms subside, after three weeks reintroduce one restricted food in two meals every day for three days before reintroducing another restricted food. By doing this, you will notice whether your body reacts to a particular food. Signs of inflammation include fatigue, anxiety, depression, skin rashes, joint pain, runny or stuffy nose, or the return of old symptoms that disappeared when you were off the food. If you get any symptoms, you need to avoid the triggering food or use it sparingly.

Vegetables, Fruits, Legumes, Nuts & Seeds
which are usually Hypoallergenic

1. All fresh vegetables (try to incorporate all vegetables such as asparagus, brussels sprouts, celery, cauliflower, cabbage, onions, garlic, carrots, beets, leeks, green beans, broccoli, leafy greens—kale, mustard greens, turnip greens, bok choy, watercress, etc.)
2. Sweet potatoes, yams, squash, pumpkin (very soothing on the gastro-intestinal tract)
3. Sprouts: sunflower sprouts, pea, and bean sprouts (especially alfalfa and red clover as they help with detoxification)
4. All fresh/frozen fruits (see exceptions below)
5. All berries, fresh or frozen (except strawberries)
6. All jams and fruit sauces of allowed fruits (with no sugars or preservatives added)
7. Brown rice, white rice, millet, buckwheat, quinoa, tapioca, teff, amaranth
8. All legumes: beans and lentils (all beans, fresh/frozen/dried), and peas
9. Raw almonds, walnuts, sesame seeds, pumpkin seeds, sunflower seeds

Vegetables, Fruits, Legumes, Nuts and Seeds
That Can Be Allergenic

1. Tomatoes, corn, mushrooms, green peppers, red peppers, bell peppers, potatoes
2. If ragweed allergy is present, then eliminate artichokes, iceberg lettuce, sunflower seeds, dandelion, chamomile, and chicory.
3. Citrus (oranges, grapefruit, and any citric acid-containing beverage)
4. Melons (often contain and promote mold growth)
5. Strawberries, peaches, apricots, apples, bananas (often have ripening chemicals)
6. Dried fruits (does not include dates, organic sulfite-free raisins, sulfite-free figs, or unsweetened dried sulfite-free cranberries)
7. Products of gluten-containing grains (wheat, spelt, rye, oats, barley), pasta, cereals, and pastry
8. Soybeans and soy products (tofu, soy milk, soy sauce, miso, tempeh).
9. Peanuts, pistachios, cashews, brazil nuts, hazelnuts, and salted/flavored nuts and seeds

Meats, Oils, and Condiments That Are Usually Hypoallergenic

1. Free-range chicken & turkey breast (best if organic)
2. Lamb (best if organic), wild game
3. Wild fish of any kind (except shark, swordfish, king mackerel, and tilefish)
4. Farmed organic fish
5. Virgin olive oil, cold or with low-heat cooking
6. Coconut oil for high-heat cooking
7. Cold-pressed sunflower oil, sesame oil, and flax oil for dressing and no-heat recipes
8. Sea salt
9. All herbs (e.g., parsley, coriander, watercress, dill, basil, thyme, oregano, garlic, ginger)
10. Most spices (e.g., turmeric, fennel, cinnamon, black pepper)
11. Spreads: nut/seed butters (e.g., almond, sesame (tahini), sunflower), bean dips (e.g., hummus)
12. Sauces: pesto, mustard without additives
13. Apple cider/brown rice vinegar
14. Sweeteners: stevia (green/brown, unprocessed) and unpasteurized honey in moderation.

Meats, Oils, and Condiments That Can Be Allergenic

1. Red meats (beef, pork, bacon), processed meats (hotdogs, salami, wieners, sausage, canned meats, smoked meats); these all contain flour, additives, coloring, and preservatives
2. Dairy (milk, cream, sour cream, cheese, butter, yogurt), eggs
3. Sea food: shellfish, shrimp, lobster, scallops, crab
4. Refined oils, margarine, shortening
5. Regular table salt (table salt is not necessarily a food allergen, it just does not have the added minerals and benefits of sea salt)
6. Avoid peppers from the nightshade family (cayenne pepper, red pepper, paprika, jalapeno, curry mix)
7. All sweeteners (corn syrup, brown rice syrup, maple syrup, molasses, brown/white sugar, glucose, maltose, maltodextrose, etc.); this includes desserts and all processed foods high in sugars.
8. MSG
9. All food additives, preservatives, and coloring

Drinks That Are Usually Hypoallergenic

1. Filtered water, at least six to eight glasses a day
2. 100 percent fresh fruit and fresh vegetable juices
3. (Herbal teas: rooibos tea, peppermint, nettle leaf tea, chamomile, licorice root, passion flower, dandelion, milk thistle, and any other herbal tea)
4. Green tea
5. Rice milk (unsweetened)
6. Nut milks (unsweetened)

Drinks That Can Be Allergenic

1. Caffeinated beverages (coffee, black tea, soda); green tea is an exception
2. Alcohol
3. Dairy (milk and other dairy products)
4. Soy milk
5. All fruit drinks high in refined sugar and added sugar

After following this diet for about three weeks, you will notice an improvement in mood, energy, and physical symptoms. My colleague, Saied Mushtagh, ND, has created delicious hypoallergenic recipes in his book *The Hypoallergenic Diet Book* available on his website http://www.hypoallergenicdiet.com.

YOUR LIVER AND EMOTIONAL WELLBEING

"Symptoms, then, are in reality nothing but a cry from suffering organs."
~ Jean-Martin Charcot

OK, NOW THAT you've stabilized your adrenal glands and minimized inflammation through diet and repairing your gut, it's time to detoxify and stabilize one of the most important organs in your body—your liver. In Traditional Chinese Medicine, your liver is considered to be your master organ. It is involved in almost every process of your body, including digestion of food, enzyme activation, hormone production, protein production, immune cell activation, storage of vitamins and iron, and blood sugar storage and regulation. Your liver is also vital for processing and detoxification of chemicals, alcohol, drugs, and cholesterol, and affects many other functions related to mental and physical well-being.

Liver and Toxins

Your liver processes toxins, which come from chemical processes in your body and from foods, drugs, alcohol, pesticides, and other environmental toxins. Your liver removes these toxins from your body by producing **bile**, which releases into your intestines and into your blood for **excretion** through your kidneys. The bile in your intestines mixes with your feces and leaves your body along with any other undigested material. Bile is also like a **lubricant** and helps your feces move easily out of your body.

Most people today have a sluggish liver due to stressful lifestyles and environmental toxins. These people detoxify less, produce less bile, and are often more prone to gas, bloating, constipation, inconsistent stools, or irritable bowel syndrome. **Constipation increases the amount of toxins retained and reabsorbed back into your body**. These toxins negatively affect hormones, neurotransmitters, and all your organs, which are all essential to emotional well-being.

Liver, Digestion and Toxin Removal

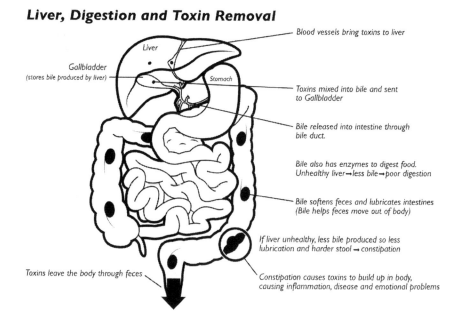

Blood vessels bring toxins to liver

Liver

Gallbladder
(stores bile produced by liver)

Stomach

Toxins mixed into bile and sent to Gallbladder

Bile released into intestine through bile duct.

Bile also has enzymes to digest food. Unhealthy liver→less bile→poor digestion

Bile softens feces and lubricates intestines (Bile helps feces move out of body)

If liver unhealthy, less bile produced so less lubrication and harder stool → constipation

Toxins leave the body through feces

Constipation causes toxins to build up in body, causing inflammation, disease and emotional problems

Increased levels of toxins also burden your organs and make them work much harder, increasing their demand for precious nutrients, which leaves fewer nutrients available for making mood-enhancing neurotransmitters. Toxins also create chronic inflammation in your body, which stresses your adrenal glands to constantly produce higher levels of cortisol. Continuously high levels of cortisol exacerbate depression and anxiety because cortisol suppresses serotonin, GABA, and dopamine, as we saw in the chapter on "Your Adrenal Glands." As you can see, poor liver function increases toxicity in your body and has a **direct** correlation with mental health. It also has a direct correlation to different diseases, including menstrual issues, low libido, irritable bowel syndrome, cancer, chronic inflammation, vision disturbances, migraines, insomnia, and many other conditions.

Liver, Lactate, Alcohol, Coffee, and Sugar

Lactate is an anxiety-creating chemical that is produced when you eat high amounts of glucose and sugars. Lactate levels increase when you eat lots of sugars, simple carbohydrates, and inflammatory foods. Your liver converts lactate back into glucose, but if your liver is toxic or sluggish, lactate levels in your blood increase rather than being converted into glucose, causing higher levels of anxiety. To minimize lactate levels in your body, do the following:

- Eat fewer refined carbohydrates, sugars, and foods you may be sensitive to.

- Avoid alcohol as it interferes with liver function and also impairs your liver's ability to convert lactate back into glucose. If you crave alcohol, you're likely low in a neurotransmitter called **GABA**, which can be remedied by using some supplements described in the chapter on "Nutritional Supplements."

- Coffee stimulates sugar to be released into your blood and also interferes with liver function, both of which increase lactate levels in your blood. Caffeine also pushes your adrenal glands to work harder without nourishing them, making depression and anxiety worse.

As you can see, high amounts of alcohol, coffee, and sugar worsen anxiety and depression, and avoiding these foods will speed up your recovery.

Liver and Your Hormones

Estrogen, progesterone, and testosterone have a profound effect on your emotions, and your liver plays an important role in regulating these hormones. Many women are estrogen-dominant, meaning they have high estrogen levels and low progesterone. **Progesterone** is an important hormone in depression and anxiety because it helps improve GABA function in the brain and is linked to **better sleep** and more **positive emotions** in women. High levels of testosterone make you feel good and reduce feelings of anxiety, leaving you less prone to depression.

With women in particular, liver imbalances cause hormones to become unbalanced, and this can cause symptoms such as irregular menstruation, painful periods, premenstrual syndrome (PMS), gas, bloating, constipation, headaches, blurry vision, breast tenderness, mood swings, and symptoms of anxiety and depression.

Other factors that alter your estrogen and progesterone balance include hormone replacement therapy (HRT) and taking the birth control pill. The chronic use of hormonal drugs depletes vital nutrients such as your B vitamins (especially vitamin B6), folate, magnesium, selenium, zinc, vitamin C, and vitamin E, increasing your risk of emotional issues.

Taking Care of Your Liver

Caring for your liver includes detoxifying your liver cells, improving their functioning and healing, and protecting them from oxidative damage caused by all the toxins they detoxify. Using herbs, diet, supplements, and castor oil packs are some of the best ways to prevent and correct liver damage.

Castor Oil Packs

Castor oil, when applied as an external pack on the skin over your liver area and abdomen, is a powerful way to flush out toxins from your liver. I have used it successfully on patients with menstrual pains, endometriosis, hormonal imbalances, constipation, and general detoxification.

- To make a castor oil pack, soak a white flannel cloth in castor oil, making sure it is wet but not dripping.

- Place the soaked cloth over your entire right rib cage, from the middle of your chest just below your right breast to the bottom edge of your ribs, spanning across to the line of your right armpit. This is where your liver sits underneath your ribcage. The castor oil will be absorbed through your skin and create a soothing, flushing effect on your lymphatic system and liver.

- Place a plastic wrap or a plastic bag over the cloth. The plastic wrap protects your clothing from the castor oil and also keeps the oil against your skin.

- Fill a hot water bottle with hot water. The water should be at a temperature that you can tolerate and that does not burn your skin. Place the hot water bottle on top of your plastic wrap. The heat will drive the castor oil deeper into the skin toward your liver.

- Leave the pack on for at least one hour while lying down, or fall asleep with it for the whole night.

- Once you are done with your pack, place the cloth in a sealable container and keep it in your fridge. Use the same cloth again the next day, with just a little more castor oil added to re-soak it. After a week of using the same cloth over and over again, wash out the cloth, because by this time the castor oil left on it will be slightly old.

- Repeat your castor oil pack daily for about two to three months. The accumulative effect of doing the castor oil pack regularly is what gives it its benefit. After a month of using the pack regularly, you will begin to notice its benefits.

Do not drink castor oil or apply it over broken skin and NEVER use it during pregnancy, breastfeeding, or while you are menstruating. If you are menstruating, have significantly loose stools, or become pregnant during this time, stop using the castor oil pack.

Liver-Healing Foods and Supplements

Foods and nutritious supplements help your liver to function better. Certain foods improve the health of your liver, some repair the damage caused to your liver by toxins, and others stimulate your liver to secrete more bile, which helps to eliminate toxins. Beets, artichoke, spinach, kale, brussels sprouts, broccoli, cauliflower, carrots, sweet potatoes, pumpkin, tomatoes, peas, beans, cabbage, parsnips, squash, yams, carrots, celery, chives, cucumber, garlic, kohlrabi, mustard greens, okra, onion, parsley, prunes, blueberries, apples, and turmeric are foods that enhance your liver's health, and they also help **reduce damage** caused to your liver by toxins. Beetroot juice, especially, is a good source of a nutrient called glutathione, which protects your liver from toxin damage.

Bitter leafy vegetables like dandelion, chicory, and rocket (arugula) stimulate your liver to **release more bile** and toxins and can easily be added to your salad. Choose organically grown foods as much as possible, since a lot of products contain pesticides, which are harmful to your body and increase toxicity. Avoid trans-fatty acids and junk food because these also increase the toxic load on your body.

Hot Water with Lemon and Cayenne Pepper

Hot water with half a squeezed lemon and a little cayenne pepper half an hour before your meals is a gentle way to detoxify your liver. This tasty drink helps your liver and gall bladder to squeeze bile out into your intestines, releasing toxins that were stored in your liver.

Antioxidants are nutrients that help to repair and protect your liver cells from damage caused by toxins. Colorful berries (e.g., blueberries and raspberries) and fresh vegetables are rich sources of antioxidants. Nutrients that are antioxidants include glutathione, selenium, vitamin A, vitamin C, vitamin E, alphalipoic acid, and coenzyme Q10. If you do not eat enough fresh fruits and vegetables, or if you live or work in a potentially toxic environment, like most of us do nowadays, you need extra antioxidants in your diet. Antioxidants are also excellent for heart health, cancer prevention, and general health.

To help your body **detoxify** better, include a high amount of **fiber and water** in your diet. Water helps your kidneys flush out toxins, and fiber binds to toxins in your intestines for easy removal through your stools. Fiber is a vital component of a healthy diet, as without being bound to fiber, a lot of toxins are reabsorbed back into your body

Herbs for Your Liver

Herbs can detoxify your liver, improve its function, and protect it from toxic damage. Most of these herbs are available in a health-food store or from your naturopathic doctor. Use these herbs under the supervision of a health professional since combining them with medicines or improper dosages may be harmful.

Milk Thistle (Silybum marianum) is a popular herb for liver health. Milk thistle contains silymarin, a powerful substance that protects liver cells from damage by toxins and other chemicals. Milk thistle also helps liver cells function better, thereby improving detoxification.

Dandelion Root (Taraxacum officinale) stimulates your liver to release more bile and is a powerful liver detoxifier. The root of dandelion is more useful for liver detoxification, whereas the leaf is more useful for kidney detoxification.

Turmeric (Curcuma longa) is a spice used in Indian cuisine and has curcuminoids, which have numerous health benefits. Turmeric protects your liver cells and stimulates your liver to produce and excrete bile. Turmeric is also antiseptic and anti-inflammatory, making it useful for infections and inflammatory conditions such as arthritis. Turmeric also seems to help with cancer and cholesterol issues, making it a truly wonderful herb.

YOUR THYROID GLAND AND EMOTIONAL WELLBEING

"Accepting someone else in their own power
is a way to your own true power."
~ Dr. Ameet Aggarwal, ND

ANOTHER ORGAN STRONGLY related to emotional well-being is your thyroid gland. Your thyroid gland produces hormones that increase your metabolism and help your cells and brain **use energy efficiently**. During adrenal fatigue the thyroid gland has to work harder to keep your metabolism going. With the lack of adrenal support, your thyroid gland gets fatigued, leading to low thyroid performance, or hypothyroidism. Using thyroid medication during adrenal fatigue can be a problem because thyroid medication increases your metabolism, which pushes your exhausted adrenal glands to struggle even more. This worsens adrenal fatigue and does not always heal hypothyroidism.

Online consultations, training, group healing seminars and healing journey safaris available
from www.drameet.com

Nourishing your adrenal glands is therefore crucial when trying to heal hypothyroidism.

Your thyroid gland produces the hormones T3 and T4, which control chemical reactions in your body and optimize the way your cells use energy. T3 is the active form, and T4 gets converted into active T3. **T3 helps your brain produce serotonin**, so thyroid health is essential for optimal mental functioning.

Your thyroid gland is activated by a hormone called thyroid stimulating hormone (TSH). TSH is produced by the pituitary gland in your brain. During adrenal stress, high levels of **cortisol suppress TSH**, which suppresses your production of T3 and T4. When cortisol levels are too high or too low, it also reduces the conversion of T4 into active T3 and desensitizes your body to the effects of T3, perpetuating feelings of depression, lethargy, anxiety, poor memory, and poor concentration.

Interestingly, the **probiotics** in your intestine convert inactive thyroid hormone T4 into active T3. T3 helps the cells of your intestinal wall join firmly together, reducing leaky gut syndrome. If the amount of probiotics in your gut is compromised or if your thyroid function is compromised, you will have less T3 available to keep your intestinal barrier intact, making leaky gut, chronic inflammation, adrenal stress, and chronic disease worse.

Another cool fact is that your thyroid gland and your liver affect each other very strongly. Thyroid hormones are **processed by your liver**, and they also affect the way your liver cells function. Low thyroid function therefore impairs liver function and exacerbates constipation, worsens digestion, and deregulates hormone balance, all of which are detrimental to your emotional well-being. Additionally, a poorly functioning liver lowers the amount of active thyroid hormone floating around in your body, worsening depression, anxiety, and other mental symptoms. So a combination of well-managed thyroid health, well-balanced probiotic levels in your gut, and a well-cared for liver is an insurance against all kinds of physical and emotional health problems.

Thyroid Hormones and Emotional Wellbeing

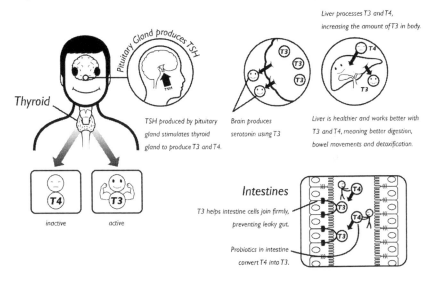

Liver processes T3 and T4, increasing the amount of T3 in body.

Pituitary Gland produces TSH

Thyroid

TSH produced by pituitary gland stimulates thyroid gland to produce T3 and T4.

Brain produces serotonin using T3

Liver is healthier and works better with T3 and T4, meaning better digestion, bowel movements and detoxification.

inactive

active

Intestines

T3 helps intestine cells join firmly, preventing leaky gut.

Probiotics in intestine convert T4 into T3.

MINERALS, ENVIRONMENTAL TOXINS AND EMOTIONAL WELLBEING

"Earth provides enough to satisfy every man's needs, but not every man's greed"
~ Mahatma Gandh

MINERALS SUCH AS copper, zinc, and magnesium affect your mood because of their effect on different organs and enzymes. **Copper** toxicity causes depression and thyroid imbalances. **Zinc and magnesium** deficiencies exacerbate anxiety.

Low levels of magnesium prevent you from absorbing and activating B vitamins, thereby offsetting adrenal health and neurotransmitter levels. A lack of magnesium also reduces the amount of calcium in your body, which makes anxiety and depression worse. **Potassium** and **sodium** levels also must be in balance for your nervous system to work well. Low levels of **chromium** distort sugar balance in your blood, leading to chronic disease and mood fluctuations. Other minerals are equally important for mental health, and if any are out of balance, your overall health suffers.

Toxic metals, especially lead, nickel, copper, arsenic, aluminum, and mercury interfere with your body's metabolism and can contribute significantly to emotional problems. **Mercury** destroys a lot of your enzymes, nerves, and other healthy tissues in your body, causing a lot of health problems. Mercury gets into your body through amalgam dental fillings, certain processed foods, vaccinations, and some types of fish like farmed salmon. If you do have mercury fillings, it would be a good idea to see a biological dentist who specializes in removing mercury fillings in a safe way. After removing mercury fillings, there still might be a certain amount of mercury floating around in your tissues. Food supplements such as cilantro and chlorella can help bind and remove this mercury. Chelation therapy, described below, is one of the best ways to get rid of toxic mercury.

Hair Mineral Analysis

Because hair is produced from cells in your body, it also contains minerals and toxins that are found in your body's tissues and the levels found in your hair somewhat reflect the levels of minerals and toxins in your body's tissues, although not accurately, because some are hidden deeply within your body's organs and do not make it to your hair. A hair mineral test, which analyses samples of your hair, gives an indication of minerals and toxic elements in your body and also gives the following information:

- Detailed explanations of which mineral imbalances you may have.

- What diseases might cause different nutrient imbalances.

- What diseases you might be prone to based on your mineral and toxin levels. For example, tests can often indicate whether you have adrenal fatigue based on the fact that your hair sodium levels are excessively high when compared to lower potassium and magnesium levels.

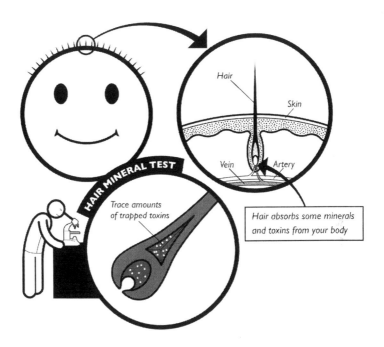

Chelation

As mentioned earlier, the hair analysis test is not a completely accurate test of the levels of toxins in your body. Ideally, it is better to measure levels of toxins directly from your body's tissues. This is possible through chelation, whereby you eat or inject medicines known as *chelating agents,* which bind to various minerals and toxic metals directly from your tissues. The chelating agent and the bound toxins are passed out of your body through your urine, which laboratories use to measure the levels of toxins in your body.

Chelation therapy is one of the best ways to remove toxic metals from your body. Depending on your health, a qualified specialist will choose a chelating agent tailored to your needs. *Dimercapto-succinic acid* (DMSA) is a popular chelating agent because it can be taken orally, whereas other chelating agents such as *ethylenediaminetetraacetic acid* (EDTA) and *2, 3-Dimercapto-1-propanesulfonic acid* (DMPS) are either expensive or need to be injected.

When using chelation therapy, always supplement with minerals such as magnesium and zinc between chelation cycles because chelation unfortunately also pulls good minerals out of your body. Nutritional products such as **chlorella** and **cilantro** will enhance the effects of chelation therapy. Large amounts of cilantro will mobilize mercury and toxins from your tissues, and chlorella will help to bind these toxins for removal from your body. I also use homeopathic medicines such as homeopathic mercury to help stimulate your body to release mercury from deep inside your tissues. I discuss the benefits of homeopathy in more detail in the section "Homeopathic Medicines."

INSOMNIA: CAUSES AND TREATMENTS

INSOMNIA IS COMMON for people suffering from anxiety and depression and makes emotional issues worse because lack of sleep stresses and exhausts the body. Most people with insomnia either find it difficult to fall asleep or they wake up frequently in the middle of the night, sometimes not being able to fall asleep again till the wee hours of the morning.

The first thing to remember while you lie awake is not to get restless or worried because this makes stress, insomnia, and emotional problems worse. When you wake up in the middle of the night or have difficulty falling asleep, remain calm and say to yourself that this is a period of resting and a chance to think of **positive affirmations**. Use this time to think of everything that went well for you during the day and everything that you could be grateful for. You can also use this time to practice some of your meditation or deep **breathing exercises** since this might be the perfect uninterrupted time to heal your mind. When you remain calm during insomnia, you will feel less stressed and exhausted during the day. I often encourage pregnant women to use this time to bond with their baby with loving words. It works like a charm.

Online consultations, training, group healing seminars and healing journey safaris available from www.drameet.com

Despite this simple advice, insomnia can actually be complicated to treat. I have listed a few common causes of insomnia and some helpful therapies for you to explore if you're having trouble sleeping.

Coffee, tea, and even green tea have caffeine and even one cup a day can keep you awake. Decaffeinated versions of these are **not** a better option because of the chemical processes used to remove caffeine from drinks. Herbal teas such as chamomile, nettle, or roiboos, which naturally have no caffeine, are a much better option.

Certain supplements, such as B vitamins and ginseng, can also be stimulating, so try taking these earlier in the day if they're keeping you awake.

Abnormal cortisol, DHEA, and thyroid hormone levels interfere with sleep. High cortisol levels at night suppress melatonin production, so definitely look at balancing your adrenal glands, healing your digestive system, and avoiding inflammatory foods, as we discussed in the chapter on your digestive system. **Adrenal nourishing herbs** such as ashwagandha and rhodiola can help correct cortisol and hormonal imbalances. Phosphatidylserine, melatonin, 5-HTP, inositol, and theanine are supplements that also help insomnia and are discussed in the section "Nutritional Supplements." Melatonin helps more for people who have trouble falling asleep whereas 5-HTP, inositol, and theanine are more useful for people who have trouble staying asleep or are not getting a deep-enough sleep. Check with your doctor before using these products because combining them with medications can be harmful.

*Low levels of the hormone **progesterone**,* which is especially common in menopausal women, can cause insomnia. Herbs such as *Vitex agnus castus* and adrenal-nourishing herbs or natural progesterone cream (used under medical supervision) can help balance your progesterone levels.

Low blood sugar *in the middle of the night* can also cause insomnia because your brain wakes up starving and looking for food, even if you don't actually feel physically hungry. Having a carbohydrate-rich meal at night without any protein can sometimes cause a fast rise of sugar in your blood, which falls quickly in the middle of the night due to large amounts of insulin produced by your body to balance the blood sugar. Eating adequate amounts of protein for dinner or snacking on almonds before bedtime will ensure blood nutrient levels do not drop too fast in the middle of the night so that your brain receives enough nutrients throughout the night. Consider using a glucometer (used by diabetics) to test your blood sugar levels if you wake up in the middle of the night.

Low levels of magnesium increase feelings of stress and can be a leading cause of insomnia. Magnesium calms your nervous system down and helps your body relax. You can take **magnesium supplements** or get it through your diet. **Epsom salts** are magnesium-containing salts that you can sprinkle in your bath, which is a lovely way to relax your body before you go to sleep because the magnesium is absorbed through your skin. I highly recommend doing Epsom salt baths because they have numerous health benefits when done regularly.

Low iron has been associated with insomnia. Even moderately low iron levels can cause insomnia and can also commonly cause restless leg syndrome. Check your iron levels and assess your diet and overall health with a naturopathic doctor if your levels are low. You could be having trouble absorbing iron through your gut or not eating enough of it in your diet. Excessive bleeding, including heavy menstrual periods, can also cause low iron levels.

Sleep apnea, or difficulty breathing while sleeping, is a common problem, especially amongst older people. Sleep apnea is usually caused by an obstruction of your airway passages during sleep, which causes you to wake up in the middle of the night or feel very tired in the mornings. Sleep apnea also deprives your brain and body of oxygen during your sleep, which leads to a fatigued feeling when you wake up. You can visit a sleep clinic where they monitor you while you sleep to see if you have sleep apnea. These clinics also offer breathing machines you can wear that prevent your airway

Online consultations, training, group healing seminars and healing journey safaris available from www.drameet.com

passages from being obstructed while you sleep. I know a couple of people who used to be extremely tired during the day and now have tremendous energy since they sorted out their breathing issues at night. I've also seen sleep apnea reduced by removing inflammatory foods from one's diet, especially dairy.

Small amounts of light and noise, even from a night-light or alarm clock in your bedroom, disrupts your sleep by interfering with your melatonin production. A nearby highway or cats meowing can create enough background noise to prevent you from getting a restful sleep. Make sure your room is **pitch black** at night to optimize melatonin production and **soundproof** your room as much as possible. Also remove any cell phones or electronic devices from your room because their electromagnetic waves interfere with your brain's restful state.

Heavy metal toxicity interferes with a lot of your hormones and organs and can cause insomnia. See the previous section "Minerals and Environmental Toxins" to learn how to test for and remove heavy metals from your body.

Activities before bedtime, like exercising late in the evening, can keep cortisol levels higher at night and prevent you from sleeping well. Eating too late at night can also cause insomnia or a restless sleep because your body is busy digesting food instead of sleeping. Avoid watching television or working on your computer at least an hour before bedtime because the light from electronic devices interferes with melatonin production. Avoid working on stressful projects close to bedtime and definitely do not keep work material in your bedroom. **Make sure your bedroom is only associated with relaxing and sleeping**.

Regular exercise during the day helps regulate cortisol levels in your body and is a great stress reliever, both of which help improve sleep quality and emotional well-being.

Castor oil packs, as described in the chapter "Your Liver and Emotional Wellbeing," detoxify your liver, which in traditional Chinese medicine is considered an important organ for sleep, stress, and emotional problems. Castor oils packs are also relaxing for your body, so do them around bedtime.

Meditation, laughter, mindful relaxation, and breathing techniques (like alternate nostril breathing, described in the "Living Well" chapter) disengage your mind from conscious and unconscious stress patterns and help your body to relax more deeply. If you find it difficult to meditate, there are some great audio-guided meditations online that walk you through powerful meditations to help you relax more. Pick up a couple if you're struggling with meditating on your own. If you wake up in the middle of the night, use this opportunity to meditate some more, think about all the things that went well for you the previous day, and think of all the things you are grateful for, including your warm bed, the sunshine of the day, the plants outside, the car you own, and the water you drink—doing these exercises is much healthier and more relaxing than becoming stressed about not sleeping well.

Treading barefoot in water for five to ten minutes before bedtime seems to help some people sleep better.

Bowen therapy and acupuncture work like a charm for many stubborn cases of insomnia. In traditional Chinese medicine, the time you wake up is correlated with an organ that may be out of balance. For example, if you wake up between 1: 00 a.m. and 3:00 a.m., your liver is likely out of balance; whereas 11:00 p.m.–1:00 a.m. is your gallbladder, and 3:00 a.m.–5:00 a.m. are your lungs. If your lungs are out of balance, it usually means there is some emotional stress or unresolved grief that you might need to process. Liver imbalance is the most typical organ problem involved in insomnia, which usually means unresolved stress, anger, irritability, frustration, hormonal imbalance, toxicity, or some food sensitivity. Some of the acupuncture points useful for insomnia, anxiety, and depression are described in the "Acupuncture and Chinese Medicine" section.

Homeopathic medicines are also great for insomnia, are very gentle on your body, and have no side effects. Some common homeopathic

Online consultations, training, group healing seminars and healing journey safaris available from www.drameet.com

remedies include *coffea* and *nux vomica*, although it's best **to see a homeopathic or naturopathic doctor** to get a more individualized remedy. Bach flower remedies can also be helpful, and there is a combination tincture sold as *Night Rescue Remedy* or similar versions of that name made by different companies.

BETTER SEX: IMPROVING SEXUAL SATIS- FACTION BY MANAGING PHYSICAL AND EMOTIONAL WELLBEING

S EX IS AN important part of many people's lives. Healthy sex, sexual pleasure, sexual satisfaction and intimacy depend on your physical and emotional health as well as on your compatibility with your partner. There's a reason this section on sexual health is after the information on how to keep your body healthy and your emotions stable. Physical ill health and emotional anxiety do nothing to improve your sex life. Now that you have understood all the factors which affect your physical and emotional health, you can grasp how they tie into sexual health.

Elizabeth was a 32 year old patient of mine. She came to me for back pain but also had vaginal spasms and vaginal dryness. This obviously made sex painful. We realized that her body was in a state of inflammation and cortisol imbalance, which was also affecting her estrogen and progesterone levels. Her hormonal imbalance was reducing her vaginal lubrication. After restoring her hormonal balance by removing inflammatory foods from her diet, repairing

Online consultations, training, group healing seminars and healing journey safaris available from www.drameet.com

her digestive health in the way I described in the chapter "Your Digestive System and Emotional Wellbeing" and detoxifying her liver, her vaginal dryness improved but the spasms did not stop.

I suspected an emotional issue with her and asked her when the spasms started. She said about 3 months ago. I then asked if she could remember any significant emotional event close to this time. 5 months ago, her boyfriend had screamed at her out of the blue when she least expected it. This wasn't typical behaviour for him and they normally had a good relationship. He had later apologized. Despite the apology, her body was still holding on to some of the shock. We processed her feelings of shock using gestalt therapy and I also gave her a homeopathic remedy for shock. 1 week later she reported to me that the spasms had disappeared.

Another patient of mine, John, had difficulty with erections after his girlfriend left him for another man. The stress and rejection from the breakup had affected his erections and burnt out his adrenal glands, which did not help his testosterone levels and libido either. After spending months working on his self esteem and trust, he finally began to have sustainable erections. We also built up his adrenal glands using certain herbs which I have described in other chapters.

Sexual issues exist for many people, and can include vaginal dryness, foul smelling discharges, lack of intimacy, painful sex, inability to have or sustain erections, feelings of inadequacy, sexual abuse, sexual shame or disturbed emotions which inhibit full sexual pleasure. A lot of our unhealthy emotions around sex come from experiences earlier on in our lives, including the way we were brought up and sometimes because of the stigma some cultures impose on sex. Some of the physical issues around sex come from having an unhealthy body but can also stem from emotional experiences, as we saw with Elizabeth and the vaginal spasms she was having. Some people experience sexual difficulties because of the medications they are on.

Inflammation, stress, a poor diet and unhealthy sugar levels can exhaust your adrenal glands and create hormonal imbalances, including lowering testosterone levels. Imbalanced hormone levels reduce vaginal lubrication, orgasmic pleasure and erectile strength. Both men and women have stronger libidos when their testosterone levels are healthy.

Your ability to experience pleasure, including sexual satisfaction, depends on feel good hormones such as serotonin, dopamine and GABA. Stress, depression, some medications and inflammation (from a poor diet, toxicity or a weak digestive system) all lower your ability to feel pleasure, so following all the dietary and stress reducing advice I've given will enhance your sexual wellbeing.

Having and maintaining erections for men depends on a strong blood flow to their penis. Smoking, inflammation and excessive sugar in your blood damages and causes plaque formation in blood vessels. This reduces blood flow to vital organs in the body, including to the penis. So if you want to have better and longer lasting erections, avoid eating the foods I have discussed which create inflammation, heal your digestive system and avoid frequent meals of too many simple carbohydrates.

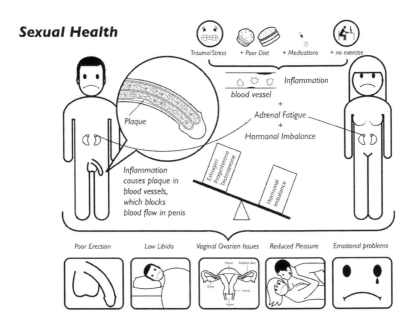

Emotional health can be vital for satisfying sex. Generally speaking, both men and women find sex more pleasurable when they are relaxed. Stress and painful emotions block our ability to let go and enjoy ourselves and our senses. Many men find it difficult to have an erection when they are stressed, have been rejected by a partner or if they are under pressure to perform sexually. I highly encourage you to resolve your stress and emotional issues with a therapist and also use some of the exercises I have given in the section "Mental Exercises to Improve Wellbeing and Heal the Past".

To encourage you further, I want to say that after spending a week resolving our emotions at our gestalt therapy retreats, when we returned home, many of us felt that we were having very satisfying sex and felt more open and sensual with our partners. Sensuality improves once we can heal our stress and emotions.

Safe sex can actually be good for your health. Most men find their stress levels reduce after sex, although this is slightly different for some women. Orgasms, in both men and women, help our body release a hormone known as prolactin, which relaxes the body and improves sleep. Sex might be something you want to consider if you struggle with insomnia. Some studies show that regular sex improves your immunity. Having frequent sex is also a form of exercise and increases your testosterone levels, which improves your confidence, mood and libido and can even reduce depression.

A word of caution: According to traditional Chinese medicine (TCM), having sex too frequently above a certain age diminishes your vitality and can cause health problems such as low back pain, weak knees and poor memory. Ancient TCM literature states the following approximate limits for sexual frequency, depending on the health of a person. These numbers refer mainly to men, since they lose a part of their vitality every time they ejaculate.

- 20 years old: 1-2 times a day

- 30 years old: once every other day

- 40 years old: once every 3-4 days

- 50 years old: once every 8-10 days

- 60 years old: once every 15-20 days

There are many other ways to improve your sex life, but that is not the focus of this book. What is important is to understand that physical health and emotional wellbeing are linked to a fulfilling sex life. I want to show you that by optimizing your wellbeing and healing your emotions, your sexual life can and will improve.

HEALTHY LIVING

"The only way to keep your health is to eat what you don't want,
drink what you don't like, and do what you'd rather not."
~ Mark Twain

I LEARNT THAT NO matter how well I ate and took care of my-self using herbs and supplements, I was still doing things in my life that were causing me harm. It really took courage to change habits that were giving me comfort only because they were familiar to me and not necessarily healthy for me.

Each and every change I talk about in these chapters really works, I promise you. Please don't make the same mistake many people do by thinking that some of these things don't apply to you or that you don't need to make changes if you don't feel like it. Change is uncomfortable for most people, and you are not an exception. Just because change might feel uncomfortable to you, it doesn't mean it is not the right thing to do. Remember, human beings are comfort-able with familiar surroundings and experiences, even if they are detrimental to their health, so take this leap of faith and try these exercises until you see the results for yourself.

Let's start with the basics of eating, sleeping, exercising, and relaxing the right way!

Eating the Right Foods

One of the most important steps I made in my life that really helped my emotions was to change my diet and exercise regularly. No matter what other therapies I went through, without a regular healthy and clean diet, there was no way I would have achieved the emotional state I feel now. Nutrients provide components that help every organ in your body to function optimally. Nutrients also help produce neurotransmitters, hormones, enzymes, and every other chemical that nourishes the organs in your body. Without adequate nutrition, your body will be more prone to emotional stress and will have more difficulty recovering from emotional problems as well.

Most of the nutrients you need are found naturally in foods, but due to diminishing soil quality and poor agricultural practices, **a lot of the foods you eat don't contain enough nutrients to be of therapeutic value**. Additionally, the amount of daily stress human beings now face requires much more nutritional support than our foods can naturally provide. You therefore need to supplement with extra nutritional supplements to make up for this lack of nutritional value in foods and for the excessive demands of daily life.

Before discussing nutritional supplements, though, let's talk about how to get the best out of your food and eat in the healthiest way.

- Eat a lot of fresh vegetables that range in color from green, red, yellow, orange, and purple. Different colored vegetables have different nutrients, which all help your body feel better, and eating different colors each day gives you the best variety of nutrients for mental wellness.

- Eat vegetables that are leafy and crunchy because they provide fiber that binds to toxins in your gut and removes them from your body through feces.

- Avoid refined and processed or packaged foods as much as possible since most of these foods are high in carbohydrates and salts and have minimal essential nutrients.

- Processed foods also contain a lot of additives and chemicals that your body has to process. These additives are harmful to your body and put an extra burden on your liver, causing increased toxicity. Your body also has to use up too many precious nutrients to process additives, which means processed foods actually rob your body of nutrients it already has.

- Avoid eating too many simple carbohydrates and sugars, which cause sugar imbalances in your blood and exhaust your adrenal glands. Simple sugars and carbohydrates also cause rapid weight gain and have the least nutritional value. If you get full on carbohydrates, it means you eat less of other nutritious foods.

"Let thy food be thy medicine and thy medicine be thy food".
—Hippocrates (460–377 B C)

Eat More Protein than Carbohydrates

The other crucial mood stabilizer I found was to keep my **blood sugar levels stable** during the day by eating more protein and complex carbohydrates with every meal and as my snacks. Protein (nuts, eggs, seeds, lentils, fish, chicken, whey, meats, tofu, yogurt, and sprouts) and complex carbohydrates (legumes, potatoes, corn, vegetables, and unrefined grains) take longer to digest than simple carbohydrates, thereby providing a slower and steadier release of nutrients into your blood. Most people eat refined/simple carbohydrates such as toast, cookies, or pastries with coffee for breakfast or snacks, which cause a sharp increase in blood sugar. The rapid rise of blood sugar forces high amounts of insulin and adrenal hormones to be produced, leading to adrenal fatigue, as we saw in the chapter "Your Adrenal Glands." Rapid insulin spikes in your body also force your blood sugar levels to drop extremely quickly and become unnecessarily low, making you feel tired, hungry, anxious, or irritable in the middle of the day simply due to **hypoglycemia**. The drops in blood sugar also cause you to crave snack foods more often, causing you to eat unhealthy foods and to worsen your health.

Ideally, your plate at any meal should consist of 50 percent green or mixed vegetables, 30 percent protein, and 20 percent carbohydrates (rice, pasta, potatoes, corn meal, etc.). You should also snack on proteins such as nuts and seeds during the day to keep your blood sugar stable.

Greens (50%)	**Protein (30%)**	**Carbohydrates (20%)**
Kale, Broccoli, Snow peas, Salads, Beetroot, Peppers, Brussels Sprouts, Spinach, Green Beans	Fish, Eggs, Chicken, Lentils, Tofu, Chickpeas, Almonds, Nuts, Seeds, Quinoa	Rice, Potatoes, Polenta, Cassava

Caffeine and Wellbeing

Caffeine stresses your adrenal glands without providing them with any nourishment. As we saw in the "Adrenal Gland" chapter, **adrenal fatigue is a leading cause of anxiety and depression**. Caffeine also blocks the action of adenosine, a brain chemical that acts as a natural sedative. Without adequate sleep, anxiety and depression get worse. Caffeine is not only found in coffee but also in tea, certain sodas, medications, and other products. Decaffeinated teas and coffees are unhealthy for you because they are made using synthetic chemical processes. It is better to drink herbal teas (see "Herbal Medicines" chapter), which you know are healthy for you.

Alcohol and Wellbeing

Small amounts of alcohol are OK for some people and can even be healthy in certain conditions, such as red wine which can be beneficial for heart disease. In depressed or anxious people, however, alcohol easily destabilizes cortisol levels and has a negative impact even in small quantities. Alcohol depletes your body of essential vitamins, especially B vitamins that are crucial for emotional well-being. Alcohol also interferes with your liver processes and blood-sugar levels, causing chemical imbalances in your blood and in your brain. Excessive alcohol interferes with your ability to work and can exacerbate financial stress, which is often a leading cause of anxiety. Excessive alcohol use can also destroy your family and social life, making your road to recovery much more difficult because you might lose the support of the people who could really help you.

Exercise Regularly

"If you don't make time for health today, you will have to make time for health later!" - Unknown

Exercise is one of the most important things you can do to feel better. In fact, without exercise, many people's chances of recovery are minimal, even if they take all the supplements and herbs prescribed in this book. Regular exercise releases the cumulative impact stress has had on your body. Regular exercise increases the amount of endorphins in your blood. Endorphins are chemicals that make you feel good. Regular gentle exercise also restores balance in your adrenal glands and cortisol levels. When threatened or stressed, your primordial brain needs to fight or flee in order to release stress and feel that it has overcome the threatening experience. **Exercise gives your brain a satisfying feeling that it is fighting or fleeing from stress**. Without exercise, your brain feels it did not respond effectively enough to stress and remains unconsciously trapped in a stressed and anxious state. Trust me, you don't want to give up on one of the most effective ways to feel better, no matter how uncomfortable it makes you feel to start.

I used to find it extremely difficult to motivate myself to exercise. In fact, I wouldn't try at all, making up excuses like "I'll do it later when I really feel like exercising", or "It doesn't feel right today", or "let me finish writing this book and then I'll begin exercising". Forget it! Whatever feelings or thoughts come up that prevent you from exercising, know that you deserve to feel better. Don't let procrastination get in your way. If you don't try and start exercising now, you'll always come up with another reason not to, and before you know it, it will be three months down the line and you'll be wishing you had started three months ago. Watch yourself and notice how convincing you can be just so you can avoid the discomfort of changing your habits.

If I don't feel like exercising or if I feel I really don't have the time, I'll make sure I do something that feels like exercise in my daily routine. For example, I'll do lunge squats to and from my shower in the morning, or I'll do a quick set of sit-ups in bed when I wake up or when I'm reading a book. I'll make sure I stretch my body, do large movements or quickly run on the spot whenever I'm doing laundry, cleaning dishes, hanging up my clothes or waiting for my food to cook. All these small activities will improve your blood circulation, help you feel better and reduce your body's resistance to starting regular exercise.

The Benefits of Relaxation

Some of us find it very difficult to take time out and relax because our subconscious mind believes it needs to keep doing what it is doing in order to feel safe and to survive. In fact, some of our brains are so hard wired and comfortable in doing routine activities that it actually feels stressful if you try and begin to relax. Your mind might think that you don't have enough time, or that something will go wrong, or that you won't manage to achieve everything you want to in life. This is ridiculous, if you look at the big picture of your life. Relaxation is meant to be a part of your life. In fact, people who take time to relax are actually more productive in the long run because they have more energy and create new brain connections which allow them to be more creative.

I never realized the power of relaxation until I forced myself to break my habits of a busy lifestyle and just take the time to enjoy myself. If you are stressed or have experienced a traumatic event in the past, taking time to relax, on a regular basis, helps your brain overcome its unconscious belief that it is still under threat. Without continuously relaxing yourself, your mind remains in a hyper-vigilant state and continues to produce stress hormones. Meditation, exercise, playing or listening to music, doing activities you used to enjoy, going for walks in nature, getting bodywork done (massage, Reiki, Bowen therapy, shiatsu, acupuncture), painting, playing with your pets, and spending time with good company all help to stop your brain from creating unhealthy and stressful nerve connections. Watching television, especially the news, **does not actually relax** your body, and can actually tire your body more because of the constant attention you give while sitting stationary. Watching TV also prevents you from exercising or engaging in healthy activities. If you want to watch television, choose comedies and inspirational programs because laughter and inspiration release endorphins in your body, which reduce stress and create long-term emotional benefits.

Healthy Sleeping Habits

Your body is programmed to rest at a specific time, and pushing your limits, like staying up late at night, strains your adrenal glands and other organs to function beyond their normal capacity. Avoiding late nights and keeping regular sleep times strengthens your adrenal glands and stabilizes your emotions. The chapter "Insomnia" goes into more detail on healthy sleep patterns, but, if you skipped that chapter because you don't have a problem with insomnia, it pays to remember this key point: **Good sleep relies on the hormone melatonin**, which is produced in high amounts during uninterrupted sleep and in complete darkness, so make sure your room is completely dark at night with as little noise disturbance as possible. Use thick curtains, and remove any night-lights or alarm clocks with electronic displays. Also remove any cell phones and electronic appliances from your bedroom because they emit electromagnetic frequencies that prevent your brain from falling into a deep sleep.

The Benefits of a Regular Routine

Your **adrenal glands** are stimulated to produce hormones accord-ing to different activities, including eating, sleeping, exercising, and working. Generally, your adrenal glands follow a circadian rhythm, producing cortisol in large amounts at 8:00 a.m. and 4:00 p.m. and reducing cortisol output between these times. It is best to keep activities such as meals, sleeping, and exercise at regu-lar times of the day to support the natural cycle of your adrenal glands. Irregular routines exhaust your adrenal glands by forcing them to readjust their hormonal output constantly.

Tidy and Healthy Living Spaces

Are you sleeping in a cluttered room, or is your house a mess? Are there negative, chaotic, or aggressive posters or images on your walls? Keeping a positive, clean, uncluttered, and healing living environ-ment allows energy to flow freely through your space and directly benefits your health. Some people have their office work in their bedroom. Trust me, this actually increases stress levels, even during sleep, because you are never separate from the energy of your work.

Read books on **Feng Shui**, an ancient practice that teaches about arranging objects in your home to optimize well-being. Put up positive words such as *love, peace, joy, friendship, wealth, harmony, and courage,* and inspirational quotes and healing pictures of na-ture, waterfalls, sunsets, etc., on your walls, cupboards, or fridges to remind your brain of peace, calm, tranquility, prosperity, and nature. Something as simple as surrounding yourself with healing scenarios can help your long-term emotional health.

Smoking and Mental Health

Smoking interferes with breathing and reduces the amount of oxygen your cells get. Oxygen is needed for your cells to function properly and for your body to feel good. Low oxygen makes your cells sick and kills them over time. It also makes you more tired, and increases the level of toxins in your body. All these factors compromise the health of your organs and reduce the energy you have to exercise, giving you less of a chance to recover completely.

Yoga

I love yoga because it changes you physically and emotionally, giving you long lasting health benefits. The type of yoga I've found best for healing depression is known as **Kundalini yoga**, which incorporates special chants, postures and breathing techniques to overcome illness. If you find a Kundalini yoga teacher in your area, stick with him or her, otherwise any other yoga class will do. I've included one yoga posture I use for reducing stress below. It is called the lion pose, also known as Simhasana. Start with this posture and seek more formal yoga classes when you're ready.

Simhasana

- Kneel on the floor with your toes pointing backward, and cross your right ankle over the back of the left ankle. Sit back onto your right heel so the soft part behind your pubic area rests on your heel.

- Place your hands over your knees and spread out your palms by stretching your fingers out as much as possible.

- Open your mouth wider and wider until it is completely wide. Then stick out your tongue as far as possible, and keep on trying to stick it out further to reach your chin.

- Then open your eyes really wide and continue to open them even wider while keeping your fingers and mouth stretched open. Once your eyes are open as wide as you can open them, gaze at the tip of your nose.

- With everything stretched and open, breathe in deeply through your nose and out through your mouth making a *haaaa* or roaring sound as you exhale, letting the air pass over the back of your throat. Continue breathing in this way while holding the pose for at least five minutes. Remember to relax your shoulders and forehead while you breathe. Stop if you feel dizzy.

- Come out of this pose by relaxing your eyes and hands and returning your tongue back into your mouth. Centre yourself by taking a few calm breaths. Practice this pose twice a day, even more if you like, especially after work to relieve stress.

Alternate Nostril Breathing

I recommend alternate nostril breathing to almost every patient I work with. Alternate nostril breathing, also known as *anulom vilom pranayama*, reduces stress, clears your mind and revitalizes your nervous system. It is promoted worldwide as being effective for depression, anxiety, insomnia, high blood pressure, asthma, allergies, and other diseases. Thousands of people around the world now use this breathing technique on a daily basis.

The Anulom Vilom Technique

- Before starting this exercise, make sure you are comfortably seated, either in a cross-legged sitting position, known as the lotus position in yoga, or comfortably in a normal sitting position.

- Using your right thumb, close your right nostril, and begin inhaling from your left nostril. At the same time, rest your index and middle finger on the center of your forehead, where your third eye is.

- At the end of inhalation, remove your thumb from your right nostril, allowing it to open, and close your left nostril with your ring and little finger as you breathe out, still keeping your index and middle finger rested on your forehead.

- Exhale fully and calmly through your right nostril with your left nostril closed.

- Next, still keeping your left nostril closed, inhale fully and calmly through your right nostril.

- At the end of inhaling, switch your fingers again, this time closing your right nostril with your thumb and releasing your ring and little finger from your left nostril.

- Exhale fully and calmly through your left nostril with your right nostril closed.

- Keep on switching nostrils in this manner and breathing for about five minutes. If you start feeling dizzy or light-headed, stop immediately, but continue your next session later in the day. You can do *Anulom Vilom* up to two or three times a day, preferably before sunset.

- The breathing sequence may sound confusing at first. Just remember these words while breathing: *In, Switch, Out...* *In, switch, out...In, switch, out...* This means that you only switch fingers after inhaling and then breathe out after switching fingers.

Anxiety-Calming Hands

If you're stuck at an airport or in a difficult situation and you're anxious or having a panic attack, a quick way to sometimes find relief is to lay one hand on your abdomen below your navel and your other hand over your solar plexus. Focus your mind on both your hands while breathing calmly. The key thing to do here is to focus on where your hands are. Your breathing will become relaxed, and the severity of your anxiety will reduce.

HOMEOPATHY, ACUPUNCTURE, COUNSELING, ENERGY MEDICINE, HERBS AND NUTRITION

"Natural forces within us are the true healers of disease."
~ Hippocrates

ENERGY CREATES MATTER, as has been explained by quantum physics. This also holds true for your body. Your physical body is created by energy vibrations creating matter. Your physical body is also affected by emotions because emotions emit energetic frequencies, either positive or negative in character. **Positive emotions encourage healthy processes** to occur in your body, such as increased immunity, better moods, less pain, and a more positive outlook on life. When you are negatively affected by an event or carry negative emotions, **those negative emotions stress your entire body**, including organs such as your adrenal glands, pancreas, liver, digestive system, and thyroid gland, all of which influence long-term emotional wellbeing.

Before we discuss energetic medicines and counseling, it is important for us to understand how your emotions exist as energetic frequencies and vibrations within and around your body. Surrounding your body, you have an energetic or vibrational field called an aura. Your emotions exist as vibrational entities within this aura as well as within your cells. These vibrations are what you sense from someone when they are angry, sad, or feeling some other emotion. Auras are well-accepted phenomena that scientists measure using Kirlian photography and other advanced devices. Some people actually see and sense auras with their eyes and other senses. Dr. Barbara Brennan, a NASA physicist, began using her knowledge in quantum physics to work with energetic healing and has written one of my favorite books, *Hands of Light*, which describes the connection between energy, matter, auras, emotions, and disease phenomenally well.

When negative emotions or experiences exist for a long time without being resolved, they continue to have a negative influence on your body. We talked a lot about the effects of these emotional holding patterns (EHPs) on your adrenal glands in the chapter "The Effects of Emotional Experiences."

Unresolved emotions cause other symptoms apart from depression and anxiety, including:

- ulcers in stressed people,

- migraines in people who have experienced trauma or sexual abuse,

- irritable bowel syndrome and loose stools in people with anxiety,

- ovarian cysts and fibroids in some women,

- different symptoms in different individuals, depending on their traumatic experience as well as on their individuality.

After resolving emotional experiences and negative thought patterns, your aura vibrates in a much healthier way. **As emotions become more and more resolved, it becomes easier for you to recover from anxiety and depression** because the stressful impact of negative emotions on your body is greatly reduced, and positive emotions begin to have a larger influence on your body. Emotions also affect your awareness and the way you perceive the world. By resolving emotions into healthier forms, you begin to develop a positive outlook on life, become unstuck from unhealthy habits, develop healthier lifestyle choices, and become better able to create other positive changes for yourself. Over time you develop an "upward spiral" of physical and emotional health.

There are many remedies that help to resolve traumatic emotional experiences and change emotional holding patterns in your aura and cells toward healthier vibrational forms that have a more positive effect on your mind and body. These include counseling, psychotherapy, positive experiences, meditation, forgiveness and positive attitudes. Energetic medicines such as homeopathic remedies and Bach flower remedies can also be helpful.

Conventional drugs are helpful in controlling symptoms of anxiety and depression and can be necessary in times of crises. However, they merely **control** your body's chemical response to difficult emotions without **resolving** the emotions themselves. They do not permanently cure emotional experiences that exist as vibrational entities in your aura and cells and that continue to have a stressful impact on your body. It is essential, therefore, to use counseling and energetic therapies, even if you are using conventional medication, so that you can clear these emotions from your energetic field and recover more permanently. Conventional drugs can be like the cast that is put on the broken bone while the bone itself heals. There is no need to keep the cast on after the healing process is complete.

The Aura, Energetic Medicine and Your Body

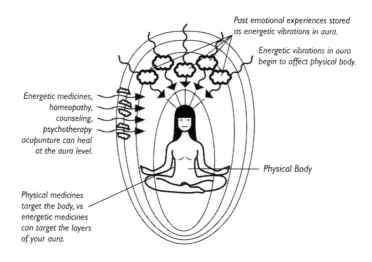

Past emotional experiences stored as energetic vibrations in aura.

Energetic vibrations in aura begin to affect physical body.

Energetic medicines, homeopathy, counseling, psychotherapy acupunture can heal at the aura level.

Physical Body

Physical medicines target the body, vs energetic medicines can target the layers of your aura.

Counseling and Psychotherapy

Psychotherapy and counseling involve talking with a therapist to resolve difficult emotions. They help you to identify, process, and release events in your life that are contributing to your current emotional state and behavior. Therapists can also give you tips and exercises to help you develop more positive emotions and behavioral responses to difficult situations.

Neurolinguistic programming (NLP), Gestalt therapy, emotional freedom technique (EFT), eye movement desensitization and reprocessing (EMDR), and quantum coaching are some of the therapies I like. They help transform and release emotional holding patterns and set your mind free, giving your adrenal glands and entire body a break from chronic stress. These therapies also help you become more authentic, enable you to act courageously from a place of truth, and help you make more positive changes in your life.

"Shelley" was a patient of mine who was sexually abused as a young teenager. She was extremely confused about the whole situation and tried to tell her father about it; however, he was emotionally unavailable. Because she had nobody to turn to, Shelley lived with her confusion and guilt for many years. She did not trust people and always interacted with people in a superficial way, hiding her shame and confusion. This took a toll on Shelley's self-esteem and social interactions. It was only when she came to see me that we allowed her to feel her confusion in front of someone (the therapist) and **created a safe space** for her to process her guilt, and all the other mixed, confusing emotions that come with sexual abuse.

After doing counseling with me for several weeks, Shelley began trusting her inner judgment and began interacting with people with more confidence. She found it easier to leave unhealthy relationships because she had more self-esteem. With her return of self-esteem, Shelley's whole outlook on life began to change, and she felt more accepted by people. Without therapy, Shelley would be stuck in unhealthy patterns without even recognizing why she couldn't control them.

Everyone has the ability to change their emotions, no matter what experiences they have gone through. Therapy helps you to develop emotional clarity and resilience so that you can take better care of yourself and create a better life. If you would like counseling sessions, I'm happy to see you personally or over Skype, which you can arrange through my website www.drameet.com.

HOMEOPATHY

"The highest ideal of cure is the speedy, gentle, and enduring restoration of health by the most trustworthy and least harmful way."
~ Samuel Hahnemann (1755–1844), Founder of Homeopathy

SCIENCE AND ANCIENT wisdom have created medicines that interact with our energetic frequencies in order to transform them into healthier or more positive frequencies. These forms of medicine are known as vibrational medicine, and the most common types are Homeopathic medicines and Bach flower remedies. Homeopathy, recognized by the World Health Organization, is a system of medicine that was developed in Germany and uses highly diluted substances given in very small doses to stimulate the body's own ability to heal itself.

Homeopathy is based on the principles of "like cures like," or the **"Law of Similars,"** which states that a disease or mental condition in a person can be cured by a substance that produces similar symptoms in healthy people when the substance is given in large or toxic amounts. The beauty of homeopathy is that it heals emotional holding patterns more permanently and is also used to treat emotional traumas that occurred in your past. Homeopathy provides you with a long-term cure rather than suppressing symptoms of illness.

"It is more important to know what sort of person has a disease than to know what sort of disease a person has."
~ *Hippocrates (460–377 BC)*

Different people react differently to events in their life and therefore develop different and unique emotional symptoms. Homeopathy uses these **unique and individual symptoms** to determine which remedy will work best for your individual emotional state. The beauty of this individualized approach is that very precise remedies are given and are therefore more effective in curing you. I describe a few remedies and their unique emotional symptoms below. A lot of these remedies can also be used to resolve any stress or traumatic experience that happened in the past.

"Mary" grew up in a broken home with her mother who had a new live-in boyfriend. Her mother was so preoccupied trying to please the new boyfriend that she neglected Mary's emotional needs quite often. Mary felt isolated from her mother, and the boyfriend did not treat Mary very kindly. The neglect was very painful for Mary to bear, so she became more sad and introverted day by day. Because she couldn't trust anyone to take care of her emotionally, she even withdrew socially from other children at school. Over time, as an adult, she never could mix with other people freely and would find herself crying easily whenever she was on her own. These symptoms of social withdrawal, crying easily when you're alone, and feeling neglected by a parent or loved one are typically associated with the homeopathic remedy *Nat-mur*. *Nat-mur* is also excellent for healing traumatic experiences stemming from separation from loved ones, including relationship breakups. After several weeks of using *Nat-mur* 200c, Mary began weeping less and felt less isolated. Her confidence grew, and she began opening up to people more, eventually finding herself a stable relationship in which she was happy.

The correct homeopathic remedy has the power to bring out the healthier form of your personality and also peels away the negative effects of emotional traumas.

Arsenicum Album (Ars) is for people who feel insecure and anxious and are often worried about their family members and financial security. They often feel worse being alone, especially at night, and feel better with company. Typical signs of people who need *Arsenicum album* are those who have fears of death, being robbed, being ill, something bad happening to their loved ones, or fearing poverty. They can be perfectionists, always tidying up, which gives them a false sense of control. I treated a patient with obsessive-compulsive disorder who would always clean around the house and had a tremendous fear of germs and of her family being contaminated by dirt (her fear of something happening to her loved ones). Within one treatment she literally transformed her life and became a much calmer person whom her husband could tolerate much better.

Natrum Muriaticum (Nat-mur) is one of the most useful remedies for depression after a loss, betrayal, or breakup from a relationship. People who need *Nat-mur* grieve for a long time and internalize their grief. They are sensitive, dislike discussing their emotions, don't cry openly, prefer to be left alone, and dislike being consoled. Because they internalize their grief, they bear resentment to others who have hurt them, and often feel mistrust. In private, they cry a lot and often cry when listening to music. People who need *Nat-mur* are also often people who appear over-responsible.

Aurum Metallicum (Aur) is a homeopathic remedy made from gold. People who need aurum feel depressed, lonely, worthless, or empty, often after a huge loss or grief. Because of this sense of worthlessness and loneliness, they are very sensitive to criticism and fear being useless. They often have suicidal thoughts or have attempted to commit suicide. They also tend to suffer from a lot of guilt, shame, or regret, and tend to blame themselves. These people may have set high expectations for themselves and failed, or made a mistake in their life, leading to their self-blame, guilt, and sense of worthlessness and depression. People who need *Aurum* also pray a lot, sometimes obsessively.

Calcarea Carbonica (Calc) is for people who are overwhelmed with work or worry and stress, which leads them into exhaustion, depression, confusion, and burnout. These people are usually responsible, hard workers who have taken on too much work and burnt themselves out. In their burnout or stressed state, they usually feel confusion, discouragement, anxiety, self-pity, depression, melancholy, tearfulness, slow thinking, and anxiety about the future, especially about their health or job security. They have difficulty hearing about bad things happening to others and are affected strongly when they hear bad news. They often feel chilly easily.

Ignatia is a great remedy to use after someone has gone through shock, disappointment, rejection, heartbreak, or humiliation. They suffer from anxiety mixed with depression and fear, often hold their tears back, keep their feelings inside when they're around people, and cry a lot when they are alone. They might sigh a lot, yawn, or feel a lump in their throat. Many also get overly sensitive and angry if they feel contradicted by someone, mainly because they have a lot of vulnerable feelings bottled up inside.

Kali phosphoricum (Kali-Phos) is one of the best remedies for nervous exhaustion. It is for people who have overworked themselves or suffered long, continuous emotional stress. They're so burnt out that they can't concentrate anymore, which makes them lose their confidence and feel even more overwhelmed, nervous, and depressed. Their nerves are so raw that they can become oversensitive to noise and light and can suffer from insomnia. People in this state also need adrenal support such as B vitamins and adrenal nourishing herbs.

Nux Vomica (Nux-v) is especially for people who are irritable. They get upset or angry easily, especially with business matters or if things are not in their correct place. *Nux-v* is also an excellent remedy to detoxify the liver and relieve chronic constipation, which also affects emotional health.

Phosphoric Acid is a great remedy for adrenal burnout and depression due to emotional stress, relationship breakups, or overwork. People who need phosphoric acid are indifferent, especially to activities they normally would enjoy, and toward family members. They also find it difficult to communicate clearly and suffer from poor memory, fatigue, and poor concentration. Phosphoric acid also helps people who lose their hair or whose hair goes gray/white after a period of grief, fear, and stress.

Pulsatilla helps people who are depressed, tearful, needy, and need to be consoled. They pity themselves or feel better when people pity them and can sometimes feel clingy or whiny. They often feel better in fresh air, after crying, or after being consoled.

Sepia is a great remedy for women who suffer from emotional issues due to hormonal imbalances. *Sepia* is also for people who are depressed and worn out, usually from overwork. They become apathetic toward family members and toward activities they used to like. They prefer to be left alone and can get angry if someone tries to console them. They are often irritable with people they are close to, especially with their partners.

Staphysagria is great for someone who shuts down or becomes depressed after suppressing their anger and emotions after being humiliated, criticized, or disappointed. They suffer from a lot of shame and lack of confidence and are very sensitive to criticism. They often appear very pleasant; however, they are prone to bouts of irritability due to the suppressed anger.

Many other homeopathic remedies exist that are useful for emotional pain. It is vital to look at individual symptoms and understand the person fully in order to select the appropriate remedy. Homeopathic and naturopathic doctors are well trained in observing other unique characteristics of a person that give them a deeper sense of what set of remedies a person needs. I always use homeopathic medicines on people with emotional issues, and I highly recommend seeing a homeopathic or naturopathic doctor for this. You are also welcome to consult with me through my website www.drameet.com.

BACH FLOWER REMEDIES

DEVELOPED BY DR. Edward Bach, Bach flower remedies are homeopathic medicines made out of special flower essences. Bach flower remedies heal emotional issues **without suppressing** your emotions because they resolve emotional holding patterns and transform energy frequencies in your aura and in your body into healthier vibrations. There are over thirty different Bach flower remedies for different emotional states such as guilt, anxiety, fear, jealousy, anger, irritability, depression, longing for the past, exhaustion, shock, and many other emotions. These remedies can help you recover emotionally much faster, manage emotional situations better, and feel you have a better outlook on life.

I always use Bach flower remedies for every patient with emotional issues because they alleviate difficult emotions significantly while the person is working on correcting their diet and making lifestyle changes. I also use Bach flowers even when someone is taking a specific homeopathic remedy because they cover a wide range of emotions and help the person heal much faster. I have listed a few Bach flower remedies that you can use in combination (a maximum of five remedies at a time) with each other or separately for any difficult emotions you might be experiencing. You can also complete the Bach flower form on my website to find the best combination of **remedies for you**.

Bach Flower Remedies for Anxiety

Agrimony is good for you if you pretend that everything is OK by putting on a brave or cheerful face despite emotional difficulties. Underneath the brave face, you are likely distressed and anxious and may stay awake at night with stressful thoughts.

Aspen is for people who are nervous or anxious, have a sense of dread, apprehension, or anticipation when there is no particular issue causing their fear. It is good if you have unexplained fears and worries for unknown reasons.

Cerato is for people who doubt their own judgment and their ability to make decisions. They ask other people for their opinions or guidance before making a decision. Cerato is great if you question your decisions a lot, have lost confidence in your own choices, and need reassurance from others about your choices.

Cherry Plum is for people who fear losing control of their mind and body. They have compulsive or impulsive behaviors that they know are wrong, but they have a difficult time controlling their actions. They sometimes fear hurting themselves or others and feel that they have to use a lot of effort to control their thoughts, emotions, and actions.

Crab Apple is for people who feel ashamed about something they have done or about something about their body. It is used if one feels unclean or contaminated by something, often after having done something wrong or after being abused. I find Crab Apple also helps if you suffer from self-abuse, anorexia, self-mutilation, or if you find yourself worrying about small physical issues such as pimples or blemishes.

Elm is excellent for you if you feel overwhelmed, worn-out, or panicky with your responsibilities because you have taken on too many commitments, or there are too many things to deal with, and you feel that you might not be able to cope anymore.

Larch is a great remedy to improve your confidence. Larch is good if you lack confidence in your own skills even though you might be capable of doing something, or if you don't try because you fear failing. It is also a good remedy if you often feel inferior to other people and believe they are more capable than you.

Mimulus is great for people who are shy and fear specific issues, such as the dark, spiders, stage fright, social gatherings, animals, flying, confrontation, people, poverty, etc., as opposed to Aspen, which is for people who suffer from unknown fears.

Olive is great for recovering from exhaustion or if you have no vitality left because you've have been through a lot, either chronic illness, overwork, divorce, financial stress, or other forms of chronic stress. Olive is great for both anxiety and depression because it helps your adrenal glands recover faster.

Pine is used for people who feel guilty and blame themselves a lot. It helps break the cycle of guilt and helps you to overcome limiting behaviors that are a result of guilt and self-blame. Guilt inhibits recovery from depression because guilt itself is a stressful emotion that perpetuates adrenal exhaustion.

Red Chestnut is for people who are anxious and over-concerned about others, especially their family. They fear that something bad will happen to a family member. Red chestnut is good for parents who suffer from anxiety because they worry about their children a lot.

Rock Rose is used if you have experienced something terrifying in your life, such as an accident, trauma, or abuse that has left one prone to anxiety. It is a good remedy to use if you suffer or ever suffered from extreme terror, nightmares, panic, or became hysterical.

Scleranthus is a great remedy for indecision, uncertainty, and hesitancy. It is for people who cannot make their mind up and may experience anguish when forced to make a decision. Such people often suffer from extreme mood swings and are not even sure how they feel about situations in life.

Star of Bethlehem is a remedy for shock and is used for emotions that stem from a traumatic event or significant grief that shocked the person. Even though the trauma may have occurred a long time ago, I often use Star of Bethlehem on most people because a lot of people have experienced some form of shock in their life. People who experience trauma often compensate their behavior because the mind does not fully cope with the traumatic event. This compensation often leads to anxiety and depression.

Sweet Chestnut is a beautiful remedy to use when you feel deep despair and have reached your limits of enduring the situation. You might have a lot of anguish and fear and feel at the end of your wits. Sweet Chestnut calms mental anguish and helps you feel hopeful. Sweet Chestnut is also great for depression, and more about this is described below under the section "Bach Flower Remedies for Depression."

Walnut helps people break away from unhealthy relationships and past attachments, go through change, and start new beginnings in a healthy manner. Change could be marriage, divorce, finding a new job, changing schools, or some other change in life. Walnut eases your transition in life and helps you feel less stress and anxiety.

White chestnut reduces mental anguish that comes from unwanted, intrusive, or repetitive thoughts and can also be helpful in paranoia and schizophrenia. White chestnut gives relief from mental arguments or consistent worries that circle your mind. It is also a good remedy to use if you have trouble sleeping because of worrying too much.

Bach Flower Remedies for Depression

Gentian helps people to recover from disappointments and failures in life. It helps people who feel discouraged and doubt their ability to succeed after a setback in life. Depression can come from disappointment, and depressed people are less likely to try to succeed again, making them even more depressed because they become disappointed by their inability to try again.

Gorse is a great remedy for depression, especially when someone feels like giving up and has a sense of despair. Gorse is for people who have given up hope and see no point in trying. Gorse encourages people to hope again, which is often the first step some people need to move forward out of depression.

Honey Suckle is for people who dwell on the past rather than focus on the present. This is a remedy for people who regret the past, dwell on old losses, or have lost someone they dearly love. It helps people move away from loss and reminiscing and helps them become more involved in their present life.

Hornbeam is for people who feel fatigue and lassitude and put things off because the thought of starting any task is too overbearing for them. This is often the case in adrenal fatigue, where your body cannot muster the will to go forward, and procrastination and apathy are your common tendencies.

Mustard is the ultimate remedy for typical depression that people often describe as a dark cloud over their head. People who need Mustard often experience gloominess, lack of joy, a *down in the dumps* feeling, and chronic sadness, usually for unknown reasons—they cannot say why they feel depressed, and their depression lifts suddenly and returns for no apparent reason.

Sweet Chestnut is useful if you feel a deep sense of despair and mental anguish, thinking that there is no way out of your depression. This state can be very tormenting, and you might feel like your soul is suffering deeply. Sweet Chestnut relieves mental anguish and gives you the strength to expect positive changes and see hope through your despair.

Willow is for people who feel sorry for themselves and live with feelings of resentment. They feel like life has been unfair to them and that others have benefitted without deserving to. They resent the successes of others because they feel that they are the ones who should have succeeded. Willow helps people move away from resentment and self-pity toward accepting that others can be successful as well.

If you would like to know which Bach flower remedies will help you, fill out the Bach flower questionnaire on my website www.drameet.com and email it to me for consultation. I usually recommend a maximum of 5 remedies at a time for them to be more effective

ACUPUNCTURE AND CHINESE MEDICINE

ACUPUNCTURE AND CHINESE MEDICINE

ACCORDING TO TRADITIONAL Chinese Medicine (TCM), your body has meridians that allow vital energy (Qi) to circulate throughout your body. Qi connects every organ in your body so that the health of one organ affects every other organ in your body. If one organ is unhealthy, every other organ is affected and so are your emotions.

By combining your physical signs with your emotional symptoms and emotional history, a TCM doctor identifies the organ that is most out of balance and uses treatments such as acupuncture and herbal medicine to help you heal at both a physical and mental level. I've covered a few TCM pictures of anxiety and depression and have listed different acupuncture points used to treat these unique pictures.

Liver Qi Stagnation

- The person is depressed, sighs a lot, gets angry easily, might have headaches, and also might have digestive issues such as gas, bloating, or constipation. Women with this condition will likely have painful menses, menstrual clotting, and breast tenderness around their menses. Acupuncture points commonly needled are Liver 3, Liver 14, Urinary Bladder 18, and Stomach 36.

Phlegm and Qi Stagnation

- The person is usually depressed, sad, cries, sighs, worries a lot, and has a poor appetite. Acupuncture points commonly used are Liver 3, Large Intestine 4, Urinary Bladder 15, Urinary Bladder 18, Urinary Bladder 20, Spleen 6, Spleen 9, Stomach 36, Stomach 40, and Heart 7.

Spleen Qi Deficiency with Phlegm/Dampness

- The person feels depressed, talks very little, worries excessively, has a stuck feeling or "lump" in their throat, and has loose or soft stools. Acupuncture points commonly used are Spleen 9, Urinary Bladder 20, Stomach 36, Stomach 40, and Heart 7.

Heart Yin Deficiency with Deficient Spleen

- The person is depressed similar to a person with Spleen Qi deficiency but also has insomnia and possibly palpitations. Acupuncture points commonly used are Heart 7, Urinary Bladder 15, Urinary Bladder 20, Spleen 6, Spleen 9, and Stomach 36.

Yin Deficiency with Empty Heat

- This usually manifests when someone has worked too hard for too long or has had years of emotional problems. The person is easily startled, talks a lot, is easily upset, has insomnia, likely has palpitations, feels hot easily, sweats at night, and is often thirsty. Acupuncture points commonly used are Urinary Bladder 15, Liver 3, Urinary

Bladder 23, Kidney 6, Kidney 3, Spleen 6, Pericardium 6, Conception Vessel 4, and Heart 7.

Liver Blood Deficiency

- The person is depressed, may have trouble falling asleep, or wakes up around 1–3 a.m., will likely have constipation, scanty menses, and possible headaches at the temples. Acupuncture points commonly used are Liver 3, Liver 8, Liver 14, Stomach 36, and Spleen 6.

- If you feel you could benefit from acupuncture, see a qualified practitioner to discuss your symptoms in detail.

Nutritional Supplements

There are thousands of nutritional supplements recommended for emotional health. Which ones do you choose? I've discussed most of them here to give you a better understanding of how they help your body. For most of my patients, in addition to repairing their gut and encouraging regular exercise, I keep it simple and usually have reliable success with a good **B vitamin-complex, fish oils,** herbs such as **Rhodiola** to restore adrenal gland function, and milk thistle to detoxify their liver.

If a patient is even slightly vitamin D deficient according to lab tests, I always supplement with **vitamin D** and encourage as much sunshine and exercise as possible. If you have trouble sleeping, consider cleansing your liver and using melatonin or 5-HTP along with acupuncture or a body therapy known as Bowen therapy, which is amazing at restoring metabolic harmony. A naturopathic doctor or nutritionist can recommend additional supplements for you based on your individual needs.

Make sure you buy good quality products from reputable health food stores or naturopathic doctors. Most supermarket brands are not strong enough. My website's products page has some of the best nutritional supplements I trust. I have also listed food sources of each nutrient so you can hopefully get most of your nutrients through food.

Calcium calms your nerves. Calcium deficiency has been linked to increased anxiety, irritability, depression, and insomnia. Heart palpitations are also associated with calcium deficiency. Calcium-rich foods include dairy products; fish (bony fish); nuts; almonds; asparagus; oats; beans; molasses; green vegetables like broccoli, mustard greens, turnip greens, and kale; nettle tea; oat straw; and kelp. People who have an allergy to dairy may find that they develop signs of anxiety when they avoid dairy products and will need to supplement with food substitutes. Calcium absorption also **depends on vitamin D**, so make sure you're getting enough vitamin D through sunlight and other foods.

Choline (Phosphatidyl choline) is a fatty acid that makes acetyl-choline, a neurotransmitter that helps with the **transmission of nerve impulses** in your brain. Choline improves memory, mood, and concentration. Reduced levels of choline have been linked to higher levels of anxiety. Choline is commonly found in lecithin, which is found in foods such as egg yolk, soy products, lettuce, cauliflower, potatoes, peanuts, and whole milk. Lecithin is also made in your body with the help of vitamin B6.

Folate is required for **energy** production in your brain. People who are deficient in folate often experience fatigue, irritability, anxiety, insomnia, forgetfulness, lack of appetite, lack of motivation, and also depression. Sources of folate include chicken, lamb, lentils, salmon, tuna, whole wheat, beans, whole grains, peas, green leafy vegetables, and fruit.

GABA (Gamma Aminobutyric Acid) is one of the most important neurotransmitters in your brain, which reduces anxiety, pro-motes sleep, and helps with rational decision-making. Low levels of GABA are directly linked with anxiety. **Vitamin B6** is crucial in the production of GABA, so consider increasing vitamin B6 before supplementing with GABA, since you might have a vitamin B6 deficiency that is causing your GABA deficiency.

Iodine is important for making thyroid hormones, which play an important role in mental health. It is important to check whether you are deficient in iodine before supplementing with it, otherwise you can have too much. A qualified health practitioner will help you to determine if you are deficient or not. Kelp and seaweed are typical sources of iodine. **Soy inhibits** your absorption of iodine.

Inositol improves the effects of serotonin and has been shown to lessen symptoms of depression, panic attacks, and obsessive-compulsive disorder. It also helps with hair growth and cholesterol reduction. Common sources of inositol include liver, brewer's yeast, meats, bananas, grapefruit, oranges, raisins, soybeans, legumes, wheat germ, unrefined molasses, brown rice, oat flakes, peanuts, eggs, and cabbage.

L-Glutamine is an amino acid essential for producing GABA. Glutamine also provides energy for your body, your intestinal cells, and your brain and improves mental clarity, concentration, and focus. We talked about glutamine's benefit in **healing your intestines** in the chapter on "Your Digestive System." Because serotonin is also produced in your intestines, healing your gut with glutamine increases serotonin production. Food sources that contain glutamine include spinach, beef, chicken, sesame seeds, parsley, cabbage, beets, and sunflower seeds.

L-Theanine stimulates the production of GABA and keeps your brain relaxed and in an alert state known as the alpha brain state, which improves mental clarity, focus, alertness, and memory. Theanine helps your body cope with anxiety and stress and protects your adrenal glands from stress. Theanine also helps you get deeper sleep. Theanine is commonly found in **green tea**, which gives it its calming effect.

Magnesium **relaxes** your nerves and muscles and is excellent for anxiety. Foods containing magnesium include dairy, fish, meat, avocados, bananas, brown rice, nuts, pumpkin seeds, sunflower seeds, sesame seeds, cereals, green leafy vegetables, and lentils.

Norepinephrine: low levels of norepinephrine are associated with depression, and excessively high levels cause **insomnia**. Certain foods like chicken, bananas, watermelon, apples, fish, and dairy products increase the production of norepinephrine in your body.

Omega-3 fatty acids are highly concentrated in the brain and are probably one of the most important nutrients for emotional well-being. Numerous studies show supplementing with omega-3 fatty acids reduces depression, anxiety, schizophrenia, and other emotional issues. Omega-3 fatty acids also **decrease inflammation** and reduce your risk of chronic disease. Alpha-linolenic acid (ALA), eicosapentaenoic acid (EPA), and docosahexaenoic acid (DHA) are the main forms of omega-3 fatty acids, with EPA and DHA providing the most health benefits. ALA is converted in the body into small amounts of EPA, and DHA and is mostly found in flax seeds, pumpkin seeds, walnuts, grains, and green leafy vegetables. EPA and DHA are naturally found in cold-water fish such as salmon, mackerel, and tuna.

Phosphatidylserine is a fat molecule that **reduces cortisol** in your body. It is excellent when elevated cortisol levels due to adrenal stress are causing anxiety, depression, and insomnia.

Selenium is an important antioxidant that improves immunity and helps your **thyroid gland**. Selenium deficiency is strongly correlated with negative mood patterns and has to be considered in depression and anxiety, especially because of its role with your thyroid. Selenium is found in fish (especially shellfish), brown rice, chicken, dairy products, alfalfa, fennel seed, ginseng, butter, molasses, garlic, liver, Brazil nuts, kelp, and sunflower seeds.

S-adenosylmethionine (SAM-E) is an amino acid commonly used to increase neurotransmitter levels of serotonin, dopamine, and melatonin. SAM-E also makes glutathione, an antioxidant that protects your liver. SAM-E is broken down into homocysteine, which is toxic and inflammatory if it accumulates in your body in large amounts, so always supplement it with **Vitamin B6, B12, and folate**.

Tryptophan is one of the most important amino acids needed to make **serotonin**. Tryptophan deficiency causes sleep disturbances, depression, anxiety, and all other mood disorders associated with serotonin deficiency. Tryptophan is found in foods like brown rice, turkey, fish, cottage cheese, green vegetables, most beans, egg whites, chocolate, oats, sunflower seeds, and pumpkin seeds.

5-HTP (5-hydroxy-tryptophan) is a supplement that is an intermediary form of tryptophan but is converted into **serotonin and melatonin** much faster. 5-HTP can significantly improve mood and sleep quality. With sleep disorders, 5-HTP generally helps when someone has difficulty *staying* asleep, whereas melatonin is used when someone has difficulty *falling* asleep.

Online consultations, training, group healing seminars and healing journey safaris available from www.drameet.com

Tyrosine helps depression and anxiety because it reduces the impact of stress on your body and improves mood and motivation. Tyrosine helps your **adrenal glands and thyroid gland** function better and is needed to produce adrenaline, norepinephrine, and dopamine. Natural sources of tyrosine include soy, chicken, turkey, fish, almonds, avocados, bananas, dairy products, lima beans, pumpkin seeds, and sesame seeds.

Vitamin A, apart from being good for your eyesight, also supports your **adrenal and thyroid glands**. It is found in liver, fish liver oils, cantaloupe, garlic, carrots, red peppers, yams, parsley, papayas, spinach, Swiss chard, kale, egg yolk, cantaloupe, and broccoli.

Vitamin B1 (Thiamine) improves nerve coordination and helps your body get energy from food. Low levels of thiamine cause restlessness, anxiety, irritability, and dementia. Because thiamine is needed to release energy from sugars and refined carbohydrates, eating too many simple **carbohydrates uses up thiamine** stores. Chronic **alcohol use also depletes thiamine** in your body. Foods high in thiamine include fish, egg yolk, brown rice, nuts, peas, whole grain, soy, tuna, sunflower seeds, and black beans.

Vitamin B3 (Niacin) is very important for nerve health, and it helps with communication in your brain. Niacin also reduces the effects of copper, which is important since high levels of copper are associated with mood disorders. Foods with niacin include broccoli, carrots, liver, wheat bran, dandelion greens, peanuts, chicken, turkey, tuna, salmon, and mushrooms.

Vitamin B6 (pyridoxine) is one of the most essential nutrients to supplement during anxiety and depression. Pyridoxine is great for **adrenal support** and nervous function and is a core vitamin for producing neurotransmitters such as serotonin, GABA, and dopamine, all essential for feeling good. Low levels of pyridoxine increase anxiety, depression, and adrenal fatigue. Foods high in pyridoxine include eggs, fatty fish like tuna, peppers, carrots, chicken, turkey, hazelnuts, spinach, sunflower seeds, and bananas.

Vitamin B12 helps anxiety and depression by reducing blood levels of **homocysteine**, a chemical produced when there is a lot of **inflammation** in your body. High levels of homocysteine have been associated with anxiety, depression, and schizophrenia. Vitamin B12 also helps your brain to function better by producing new nerve cells. It has been shown to help chronic fatigue, low energy, adrenal fatigue, heart palpitations, and poor memory, all of which are often symptoms in depression and anxiety. Foods high in B12 include fatty fish, sardines, mussels, lamb, eggs, and yogurt.

Vitamin C combats stress, anxiety, and depression because it strengthens your **adrenal glands** and is needed to produce adrenaline. It is also a powerful antioxidant that protects your body from toxins and free radical damage, ensuring all your organs work optimally. Food sources of vitamin C include papaya, citrus fruits, broccoli, strawberries, peppers, kiwi fruit, and guava.

Vitamin D plays a key role in combating depression and other chronic diseases, and its deficiency has been directly linked to depression. Vitamin D production in your body is increased through direct exposure to sunlight. In recent years, because of tall buildings, driving cars, and living indoors, everyone's exposure to sunlight is significantly less. Most of us also use chemical soaps, which remove oils from our skin that make Vitamin D from sunlight. It is better to reduce using soap on large areas of your body and use it mainly on pubic and armpit areas where sweat and smells accumulate. Vitamin D and sunlight also **increase serotonin** levels and increase your body's absorption of calcium, which calms you down. Food sources of Vitamin D include fatty fish, liver, dandelion greens, butter, and egg yolk. Vitamin D is toxic to your liver in high amounts, so consult your doctor before supplementing with it.

Zinc is a fantastic mineral that has a calming effect and is essential for the health of your **adrenal glands**. In fact, the highest concentration of zinc in your body is found in your adrenal glands. Zinc helps your body absorb B vitamins and helps your adrenal glands produce hormones. Zinc is also crucial for strengthening your immune system. Foods high in zinc include oysters, egg yolk, shellfish, pumpkin seeds, sunflower seeds, soy, wheat germ, nuts, and meats.

If you're wondering which foods to start with, consider having the following foods in most of your meals:

- Lots of broccoli and green leafy vegetables like kale and spinach, which are high in folate, magnesium, and antioxidants

- Salmon and other oily fish, rich in omega-3 fatty acids and vitamin D

- Turkey, rich in amino acids such as tryptophan and tyrosine

- Bananas, rich in tryptophan, magnesium, and potassium

- Lots of nuts and seeds, which are rich in omega-3 fatty acids and magnesium

Herbal Medicines

I use herbal medicines in a variety of ways to treat emotional problems depending on what your underlying cause is. We have already discussed some ways in which herbs can be effective at improving general health. You may remember, I recommended using herbs such as rhodiola or ginseng (discussed in "Your Adrenal Glands and Emotional Wellbeing" chapter), to help your adrenal glands and provide the most long-term benefits for anxiety and depression. I also mentioned herbs that heal or detoxify your liver (in "Your Liver and Emotional Wellbeing" chapter) and your digestive system since these two systems affect your emotional health.

While stabilizing your adrenal glands and restoring your digestive health, you could also use herbs to temporarily elevate your mood (antidepressant) or reduce anxiety (anxiolytic) and insomnia, which I have covered below. When using herbal remedies, is it important to look at factors such as lifestyle, emotional experiences, diet, environmental toxicity, liver health, digestive health, and other systems that affect mental health.

Please note that some of these herbs can be extremely dangerous if misused, if used for too long, if combined with other medications and other herbs, or if used during pregnancy or lactation. I have not indicated which herbs are harmful in pregnancy or what their toxic side effects are, so **make sure you consult with your doctor before using any herb**.

Black Pepper (Piper Nigrum) stimulates your metabolism and increases circulation. It can help alleviate depression due to its stimulating effects.

Cayenne pepper (Capsicum frutescens), funnily enough, is also useful in depression because of its stimulating properties. It could be added to your food on a regular basis, especially during cold winter months when depression increases for many people.

Chamomile (Matricaria recutita) has a **sedative and calming** effect so it helps with sleep, anxiety, and irritability. Being antispasmodic, it also soothes your digestive system if you have cramps and indigestion. Using chamomile for too long can cause allergies to chamomile in some people, so I generally recommend using chamomile tea for two weeks and taking a break for about one month to reduce chances of allergies.

Green Tea (Camellia sinensis) contains a nutrient called L-Theanine, which improves mental clarity, focus, alertness, and memory; stimulates the production of GABA; and has a **calming effect** on your brain. Theanine helps your body cope during stressful periods by reducing the harmful effects of stress on your body. Theanine also helps induce deeper sleep in people who feel restless at night. Many cultures traditionally remove the caffeine from green tea by steeping the leaves in hot water for about one minute, pouring the water away, and adding hot water to the leaves again.

The first brew removes the caffeine from the leaves, and the second brew leaves you with the benefits of all the other nutrients in green tea.

Indian Snakeroot (Ajmaline, Rauwolfia serpentina) is immensely beneficial for stress and is fantastic for people who cannot **sleep** because of **stress**. Mahatma Gandhi used to chew on its root or drink *Ajmaline* as a tea to help him sleep well. *Ajmaline* also reduces blood pressure and is used in hypertension.

Jamaica Dogwood (Piscidia erythrina) is a powerful sedative and a muscle relaxant. It is best used for anxiety that has a lot of nervousness, **insomnia**, and restlessness. Jamaica Dogwood can also be used as a pain killer. Be careful with this herb because it can be toxic in large amounts.

Kava Kava (Piper methysticum) is an herb that is native to the Pacific Islands and is used in ceremony, socially, and also for medicinal purposes. Kava Kava is stimulating and calming and is also an aphrodisiac. It is used to treat anxiety and mild symptoms of depression because of its uplifting effects.

Lemon Balm (Melissa officinalis) is a gentle, **relaxing**, and slightly uplifting herb and is used for both anxiety and depression. Lemon balm makes a pleasant tea and also has a soothing effect on your stomach and intestines, making it useful for digestive complaints arising from anxiety.

Passion Flower (Passiflora incarnata) is a powerful herb that calms your nerves and helps with **sleep**. Passionflower is one of the stronger herbs used to induce sleep and is excellent to prevent nervousness that comes from insomnia or exhaustion.

Peppermint tea (Mentha piperita) calms your mind during stress and also soothes digestive cramps, gas, and bloating.

St. John's Wort (Hypericum perforatum) is one of the most common herbs used for mild to **moderate depression**. It is also useful for anxiety and insomnia but is not used for severe depression. St. John's Wort interacts adversely with many medications and causes serotonin toxicity if taken with serotonin reuptake inhibitors antidepressants (SSRIs), so consult your physician before using it with any medication.

Valerian (Valeriana officinalis) calms nervousness and is good for depressed people who feel a constant low-grade **nervousness** rather than extreme anxiety. It also helps with sleep, especially when the insomnia is due to nervousness and worrying thoughts.

Aromatherapy

Aromatherapy uses the scents of various herb oils to heal your mind.

Oils that are useful for anxiety, stress, and depression include:

Cedarwood,
Sandalwood
Bergamot
Jasmine
Lavender
Chamomile
Clary sage,
Peppermint,
Juniper
Geranium
Neroli (orange blossom)
Melissa
Patchouli
Basil,
Ylang ylang
Lemon

Lavender, marjoram, geranium, mandarin, and cardamom are helpful for sleep.

Many aromatherapy oils can be harmful in pregnancy, so always check with your doctor before using them if you are pregnant or trying to conceive. In particular basil, bay, comfrey, hyssop, juniper, marjoram, melissa, and clary sage should all be avoided in pregnancy.

Aromatherapy oils are extremely strong and concentrated and cannot be applied directly to the skin. Instead, they are diluted in oils such as almond oil and then applied to the skin, usually through massage. Aromatherapy oils can also be added to your bath or put in a vaporizer or humidifier to dispense their aroma into the air so you can breathe in their healing scent.

Aromatherapy is useful because it helps you to feel good and lessens the stress on your body caused by different emotions. By reducing emotional stress and having more positive thoughts, your body recovers faster from fatigue and illness, and it becomes easier for you to take more positive steps in life.

DRUGS USED IN ANXIETY AND DEPRESSION

"He who takes medicine and neglects to diet
wastes the skill of his doctors."
~ Chinese Proverb

W HEN TREATING EMOTIONAL disease, most conventional doctors or psychiatrists prescribe drugs that alter the levels of neurotransmitters in your body. Even though conventional medicines may control symptoms of anxiety and depression, they often do not cure or treat the root cause. That being said, conventional medicines can be necessary and lifesaving, especially in situations where you are at risk of harming yourself, committing suicide, or cannot carry out basic activities because of your emotions.

While taking medication, you must also consider why you are prone to emotional issues in the first place in order to heal at a deeper level. By treating the root cause and improving your overall health, you will likely improve the effect of your medications and can also become less dependent on medication as you become more emotionally resilient.

I have described a few drugs commonly used for anxiety and depression below. Some are not used anymore because of side effects and because other drugs are more effective. Examples of the different drugs are given with their trade names in parenthesis ().

It is extremely important to consult with your physician before changing the dose or stopping any medication. Changing dosage or stopping these medicines without appropriate supervision can result in a relapse or a worsening of your symptoms.

Benzodiazepines enhance the effects of GABA in your brain and are used for anxiety, insomnia, panic disorders, obsessive compulsive disorder (OCD), and alcohol withdrawal. Side effects of benzodiazepines include drowsiness, dizziness, sexual dysfunction, decreased alertness, and decreased concentration. Coming off benzodiazepines too quickly can cause significant side effects, including increased anxiety and tremors. Some examples of benzodiazepines include Diazepam (Valium), Lorazapam (Ativan), Triazolam (Halicon), and Alprazolam (Xanax).

Bupropion (Wellbutrin, Zyban) is an antidepressant that increases levels of norepinephrine, serotonin, and dopamine in your brain by preventing their reuptake by other tissues. Buproprion is commonly used for depression, for quitting smoking, and for seasonal affective disorder (SAD). Side effects of Bupropion include seizures, nausea, insomnia, tremors, excessive sweating, and ringing in your ears (tinnitus).

Selective Norepinephrine Reuptake Inhibitors (SNRIs) increase levels of serotonin and norepinephrine in your brain by preventing their reuptake. SNRIs are used for anxiety, panic disorders, depression, and OCD. Side effects of SNRIs include insomnia, tremors, anxiety, abnormal dreams, fatigue, high blood pressure, sexual dysfunction, digestive troubles, and other side effects that are listed on the packaging. Examples of SNRIs include Venlafaxine and Duloxetine.

Selective Serotonin Reuptake Inhibitors (SSRIs) prevent the reuptake and breakdown of serotonin and hence increase serotonin levels in your brain. SSRIs are commonly used to treat depression, bulimia, anorexia, social phobia, anxiety, and obsessive-compulsive disorder (OCD). Side effects of SSRIs include, but are not limited to, sexual dysfunction, tremors, nervousness, nausea, increased risk of suicide (especially in children and young adults), drowsiness, and sleep difficulties. Examples of SSRIs include Fluoxetine (Prozac), Sertraline (Zoloft), Paroxetine (Paxil), and Citalopram.

The important thing to remember is that while conventional medicines can be valuable to provide short-term relief from symptoms, they should not be seen as a long-term solution. Work with your doctor to address the causes of emotional issues and to manage your medications while finding lasting solutions and coping strategies.

SUMMARY

We have covered a lot of ground in this book, and if you've read this far, now is a good time to go back over the sections that apply to you and start to implement the strategies that are most relevant to your circumstances. Here are some of the key points you should keep in mind as you do so.

To regain emotional strength, look at emotional or energetic areas of your life, including past experiences, physical issues in your body, and lifestyle factors that affect emotional health.

To resolve emotional experiences and energetic holding patterns, consider using:

- Bach flower remedies and homeopathic medicines

- Counseling, psychotherapy, or emotional freedom technique

- Acupuncture, Bowen therapy, or some other body therapy

- Meditation, positive visualization, and some of the other exercises described in this book to resolve emotional experiences

To treat your physical body, consider the following:

- Stabilize your adrenal glands using herbs, supplements, regular routines, healthy sleeping habits, and regular deep breathing techniques

- Heal your digestive system using herbs, probiotics and supplements and reduce inflammatory foods, drugs, and alcohol

- Detoxify your liver using herbs or supplements and eat lots of green vegetables and fiber to remove toxins from your digestive system.

- Eat correctly by minimizing sugars, avoiding junk food, eating nutritious foods, and ensuring you're eating enough protein

- Exercise or do yoga regularly to detoxify your body, increase oxygen flow to your tissues, stabilize your adrenal glands, and stabilize your brain chemicals

- Use physical therapies such as acupuncture, massage, or Bowen therapy, which have relaxing and other healthy benefits for your entire body.

I hope you gained something useful from this book. I think it is important to invest in yourself and live life enjoyably and as fully as you can make it. The more we can empower and help each other to do that, the better we will all feel.

If you like what you read in this book and would like a consultation, to train with me, to go on a healing journey safari, or have me work with your organization, please contact me through ameet@drameet.com or through www.facebook.com/drameet and www.drameet.com. I wish you the best in life.

"It is health that is real wealth and not pieces of gold and silver."
—Mahatma Gandhi

HEALING THROUGH INSPIRATION AND TRANSFORMATIONAL AWARENESS

PARADIGM SHIFTS ARE a way of looking at the world, situations, and your own personal experiences in a different way. They help you shift your perspective, behavior, and physiological response to the world inside and around you. I sometimes feel that a shift in perspective allows for change in our emotions, which inevitably brings about healing. I am including a few of my thoughts below to inspire you to allow changes in your emotions and in your life.

Healing is an aspect of letting go of perceived self so that true self may emerge free of disease.

All emotional experiences begin a physiological process in your body. For every act, emotion, and expression of love, self-love, self-forgiveness, and forgiveness toward another, your body reengages toward another physiological process, closer to its original process, its healthiest process...

Just like the unseen currents create winds, which you can feel, which move a leaf, which you can see, so do unseen thoughts create emotions, which you can feel, which create disease or healing, which you can see. We are all nature...

Accept, love and include every negative belief, thought and dark part of yourself as a full and integral part of your higher and lighter self because then it all begins to dissolve into the lighter higher conscious part of you; just like the way darkness in a room melts away when a candle is brought in... It can't be the other way around... Darkness does not put a candle out...

The mathematics of disease

An experience creates a movement of energy. The movement of energy gains momentum, depending on the intensity of the experience. If left unhindered, the energy's momentum increases enough to create matter, which manifests as physical symptoms in your body. The longer you wait to intervene, the more work is required to reverse the momentum and undo disease. Very serious diseases and cellular degenerative diseases could be the momentum of energetic disease overcoming your body's resilience to recover itself from the intensity of the experience. By mentally engaging with and accepting the experience of the event that manifested the disease, we actually match our awareness to where the energy of the experience is, and time collapses so that the momentum of diseased energy dissolves into the present moment, thus freeing the mind and body from struggling against it and from manifesting symptoms.

If we didn't fully include ourselves in a difficult or stressful situation because we felt threatened or intimidated or something else, then we remain in a subconsciously stressed state, which alters our perception and behaviors. Until we realize the compensation, we create disease and disharmony in our lives.

Your vulnerability is from where your true power begins

Tears are often a sign of truth and not of weakness...

Allow yourself to succumb to yourself, for therein lies the peace and self-recognition.

The fear of change could be the fear of love...

Sometimes emotional pain is made up of the opinion you have of another person and their behavior. How many opinions do you hang on to? Let go and experience freedom.

Sometimes habit feels like intuition. It keeps you stuck in the familiar. It guides you to keep safe and avoid change. It doesn't necessarily bring what is best for you. Know the difference between guidance and intuition and habit and change...Step out of familiar and guidance and tolerate change till it becomes easy...

Procrastination could be the avoidance of risking change...

Confidence comes more from doing, not by not doing...

What entity is mind then, if it interferes with universal guidance?

A language engages our consciousness so that we think in a certain way. If we were to think in a different language, our consciousness would be different. If we would think in terms of in light and love, we would be free...

If your emotions are calm, the way you interpret your experiences will be calm. The same goes if your emotions are loving, peaceful, or any other way!

Bad habits occur when we become numb to the experiences that created them. Become aware...You have choice.

The advancement in medicine of the future will be love...

Online consultations, training, group healing seminars and healing journey safaris available from www.drameet.com

REFERENCES

What is Anxiety and Depression?

- Strande, Alex, ND, PhD. September/October 2001. "Lifting Depression." *Awareness Magazine.* Accessed November 25th 2011 from http://www.simplyhealingclinic.com/articles/lifting_depression.html.

How Your Physical Body Affects Emotional Health

- Morse, Trish. "Hormones affect anxiety and depression." Retrieved November 25th 2011 from http://www.hormone-jungle.com/depression.php.

- Pataracchia, Dr. Raymond J. BSc, ND. "Orthomolecular treatment for depression, anxiety, and behavior disorders." Accessed September 21, 2011 from http://www.nmrc.ca/pages/Nutritional_Treatment_of_Mental_Health.cfm.

- Mota-Pereira, J. "Moderate exercise improves depression parameters in treatment-resistant patients with major depressive disorder." *J Psychiatr Res.* August 11, 2011; 45(8): 1005-11. Accessed September 21, 2011. MEDLINE® is the source for the citation and abstract of this record.

- Hallberg, L. "Exercise-induced release of cytokines in patients with major depressive disorder." *J Affect Disord.* October 1, 2010; 126(1-2): 262-7. Accessed September 21, 2011. MEDLINE® is the source for the citation and abstract of this record.

Mental Exercises to Improve Wellbeing and Heal The Past

- Seligman, M. Ph.D. Authentic Happiness: Using the New Positive Psychology to Realize Your Potential for Lasting Fulfillment. New York: The Free Press, 2002.

- Yook, K. "Intolerance of uncertainty, worry, and rumination in major depressive disorder and generalized anxiety disorder." *J Anxiety Disord.* August 1, 2010; 24(6): 623-8. MEDLINE® is the source for the citation and abstract of this record.

- The effects of rumination and negative cognitive styles on depression: a mediation analysis. Lo CS - *Behav Res Ther.* April 1, 2008; 46(4): 487-95. Accessed September 21, 2011. MEDLINE® is the source for the citation and abstract of this record.

- Your Adrenal Glands and Emotional Wellbeing

- Vreeburg, S. A. "Major depressive disorder and hypothalamic-pituitary-adrenal axis activity: results from a large cohort study." *Arch Gen Psychiatry.* June 1, 2009; 66(6): 617-26. Accessed September 21, 2011. MEDLINE® is the source for the citation and abstract of this record.

- Ahrens, T. "Pituitary-adrenal and sympathetic nervous system responses to stress in women remitted from recurrent major depression." *Psychosom Med.* May 1, 2008; 70(4): 461-7. Accessed September 21, 2011. MEDLINE® is the source for the citation and abstract of this record.

- Aan het Rot, M. "Neurobiological mechanisms in major depressive disorder." *CMAJ.* February 3, 2009; 180(3): 305-13. Accessed September 21, 2011. MEDLINE® is the source for the citation and abstract of this record.

- Handwerger, K. "Differential patterns of HPA activity and reactivity in adult posttraumatic stress disorder and major depressive disorder." *Harv Rev Psychiatry.* January 1, 2009; 17(3): 184-205. Accessed September 21, 2011. MEDLINE® is the source for the citation and abstract of this record.

- Interview with David Zava, Ph.D. "Cortisol Levels, Thyroid Function and Aging. How cortisol levels affect thyroid function and aging." Originally published in the John R. Lee, MD Medical Letter. Accessed May 29, 2012 from http://www.virginiahopkinstestkits.com/cortisolzava.html.

- Mushtagh, Dr. Saied, ND. *The Hypoallergenic Diet Book.* Toronto 2006.

- Schizandra chinensis, "Phytochemicals." Accessed September 21, 2011 from http://www.phytochemicals.info/plants/schizandra.php.

Your Digestive System and Emotional Wellbeing

- Maes, M. "The gut-brain barrier in major depression: intestinal mucosal dysfunction with an increased translocation of LPS from gram negative enterobacteria (leaky gut) plays a role in the inflammatory pathophysiology of depression." *Neuro Endocrinol Lett.* February 1, 2008; 29(1): 117-24. Accessed September 21, 2011. MEDLINE® is the source for the citation and abstract of this record.

- Quigley, E. M. "Small intestinal bacterial overgrowth." *Infect Dis Clin North Am.* December 1, 2010; 24(4): 943-59, viii-ix. Accessed September 21, 2011. MEDLINE® is the source for the citation and abstract of this record.

- Mattsen, Jonn. 2002. *Eating Alive*. Vancouver: Goodwin Books, Ltd.

- Yang, C. F. "High prevalence of multiple micronutrient deficiencies in children with intestinal failure: a longitudinal study." *J Pediatr.* July 1, 2011; 159(1): 39-44.e1. Accessed September 21, 2011. MEDLINE® is the source for the citation and abstract of this record.

- El-Tawil, A. M. "Zinc supplementation tightens leaky gut in Crohn's disease." *Inflamm Bowel Dis.* February 1, 2012; 18(2): E399. Accessed September 21, 2011. MEDLINE® is the source for the citation and abstract of this record.

- Kirby, M. "Nutritional deficiencies in children on restricted diets." *Pediatr Clin North Am.* October 1, 2009; 56(5): 1085-103. Accessed September 21, 2011. MEDLINE® is the source for the citation and abstract of this record.

- Canadian College of Naturopathic Medicine. *The Hypoallergenic Diet*. Robert Schad Naturopathic Clinic.

Your Liver and Emotional Wellbeing

- Johnson, P. L. "Neural pathways underlying lactate-induced panic." *Neuropsychopharmacology.* August 1, 2008; 33(9): 2093-107. Accessed September 21, 2011. MEDLINE® is the source for the citation and abstract of this record

- *Anxiety. Healthy Lifestyle.* Accessed on July 16, 2012 from http://www.fitness-health.co.uk/anxiety-treatment.htm.

- Sellman, Sherrill. "Hormones and moods: Understanding depression and anxiety in women." Accessed on

November 25, 2011 from http://www.encognitive.com/node/6988.

- Cass, Dr. Hyla. Seminar on Addictions, Audio Webinar. Accessed May 2013 from http:7days7docs.com.

- Milad, M. R. "The influence of gonadal hormones on conditioned fear extinction in healthy humans." *Neuroscience.* July 14, 2010; 168(3): 652-8. Accessed September 21, 2011. MEDLINE® is the source for the citation and abstract of this record.

- van Veen, J. F. "The effects of female reproductive hormones in generalized social anxiety disorder." *Int J Psychiatry Med.* January 1, 2009; 39(3): 283-95. Accessed September 21, 2011. MEDLINE® is the source for the citation and abstract of this record.

Your Thyroid Gland and Emotional Wellbeing

- Durrant-Peatfield, Dr. Barry. 2006. Your Thyroid and How to Keep it Healthy. Hammersmith Press Limited.

- Hidal, J. T., and M. M. Kaplan. 1988. "Inhibition of thyroxine 5'-deiodination type II in cultured human placental cells by cortisol, insulin, 3', 5'-cyclic adenosine monophosphate, and butyrate." *Metabolism.* 37(7):664-8.

- Shames, Drs. Richard and Karilee. 2002. *Thyroid Power. 10 Steps to Total Health.* William Morrow Paperbacks.

- Malik, R, and H. Hodgson. "The Relationship between the thyroid gland and the liver." *QJ Med.* 2002; 95:559-569.

- Martin, P., D. Brochet, P. Soubrie, and P. Simon. September 1985. "Triiodothyronine-induced reversal of learned helplessness in rats.". *Biol. Psychiatry.* **20** (9): 1023–5. doi:10.1016/0006-3223(85)90202-1. PMID 2992618.

Healthy Living

- Whalen, D. J. "Caffeine consumption, sleep, and affect in the natural environments of depressed youth and healthy controls." *J Pediatr Psychol.* May 1, 2008; 33(4): 358-67. Accessed September 21, 2011. MEDLINE® is the source for the citation and abstract of this record.

- Mota-Pereira, J. "Moderate exercise improves depression parameters in treatment-resistant patients with major depressive disorder." *J Psychiatr Res.* August 1, 2011; 45(8): 1005-11. MEDLINE® is the source for the citation and abstract of this record.

Better Sex: Improving Sexual Satisfaction by managing Physical and Emotional Wellbeing

- Robinson, K. Sex & Relationships. WebMD. Retrieved on 31st October 2013 from http://www.webmd.com/sex-relationships/guide/sex-and-health

- Kassam, N. ND. Traditional Chinese Medicine Class Notes. CCNM (2006).

Bach Flower Remedies

- Bach Flower Questionnaire, Canadian College of Naturopathic Medicine.

- Bach, Dr. Edward. Bach Flower Remedies and Other Remedies. (1933)

Acupuncture and Chinese Medicine

- Zhang, Z. J. "The effectiveness and safety of acupuncture therapy in depressive disorders: systematic review and meta-analysis." *J Affect Disord.* July 1, 2010; 124(1-2): 9-21. Accessed September 21, 2011. MEDLINE® is the source for the citation and abstract of this record.

- Bongiorno, Dr. Peter , ND, LAc. *Healing Depression, Integrated Naturopathic and Conventional Therapies.* Toronto: CCNM Press, Inc. 2010.

Nutritional Supplements

- Balch, Phyllis A., cnc, and James F. Balch, MD. *Prescription for Nutritional Healing*, 3rd Edition. New York: Avery, 2000.

- Wong-Goodrich, S. J. "Spatial memory and hippocampal plasticity are differentially sensitive to the availability of choline in adulthood as a function of choline supply in utero." *Brain Res.* October 27, 2008; 1237: 153-66. Accessed September 21, 2011. MEDLINE® is the source for the citation and abstract of this record.

- Zhao, G. "Use of folic acid and vitamin supplementation among adults with depression and anxiety: a cross-sectional, population-based survey." *Nutr J.* January 1, 2011; 10: 102. Accessed September 21, 2011. MEDLINE® is the source for the citation and abstract of this record.

- Sánchez-Villegas, A. "Association between folate, vitamin B(6) and vitamin B(12) intake and depression in the SUN cohort study." *J Hum Nutr Diet.* April 1, 2009; 22(2): 122-33. Accessed September 21, 2011. MEDLINE® is the source for the citation and abstract of this record.

- Pollack, M. H. "High-field MRS study of GABA, glutamate and glutamine in social anxiety disorder: response to treatment with levetiracetam." *Prog Neuropsychopharmacol Biol Psychiatry.* April 1, 2008; 32(3): 739-43. Accessed September 21, 2011. MEDLINE® is the source for the citation and abstract of this record.

- Fux M, J Levine, A. Aviv, and R. H. Belmaker. 1996. "Inositol treatment of obsessive-compulsive disorder." *American Journal of Psychiatry.* 153(9):1219-21 Accessed September 21, 2011. MEDLINE® is the source for the citation and abstract of this record.

- Kakuda T, A. Nozawa, T Unno, et al. 2000. "Inhibiting effects of theanine on caffeine stimulation evaluated by EEG in the rat." *Biosci Biotechno Biochem;* 64:287-293. Accessed September 21, 2011. MEDLINE® is the source for the citation and abstract of this record.

- Parker, G. "Mood effects of the amino acids tryptophan and tyrosine: 'Food for Thought'" III. *Acta Psychiatr Scand.* December 1, 2011; 124(6): 417-26. Accessed September 21, 2011. MEDLINE® is the source for the citation and abstract of this record.

- Stewart, R. "Relationship between vitamin D levels and depressive symptoms in older residents from a national survey population." *Psychosom Med.* September 1, 2010; 72(7): 608-12. Accessed September 21, 2011. MEDLINE® is the source for the citation and abstract of this record.

- Mushtagh, Dr. Saied, ND. *The Hypoallergenic Diet Book.* Toronto 2006.

- Larzelere, M. M. "Complementary and alternative medicine usage for behavioral health indications." *Prim Care.* June 1, 2010; 37(2): 213-36. Accessed September 21, 2011. MEDLINE® is the source for the citation and abstract of this record

- Prousky, Dr. Jonathan ND. Clinical nutrition notes (2006), Canadian College of Naturopathic Medicine.

Herbal Medicines

- Saunders, P., PhD, ND, DHANP. Botanical Medicine Class Notes. CCNM (2006).

Drugs used in Anxiety & Depression

- Mental Health Medications. National Institute of Mental Health. Accessed September 20th 2012 from http://www.nimh.nih.gov/health/publications/mental-health-medications/index.shtml.

Made in the USA
Charleston, SC
14 February 2014